I Walk With God

The Autobiography of Marjorie Clevenger Hinkle

Margie Hinkle

Compiled and Edited by Sherry Hatchett & Bonnie Holmes

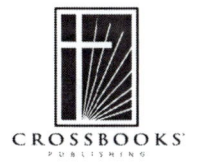

CROSSBOOKS

CrossBooks™
A Division of LifeWay
1663 Liberty Drive
Bloomington, IN 47403
www.crossbooks.com
Phone: 1-866-879-0502

©2010 Margie Hinkle. All rights reserved.

No part of this book may be reproduced, stored in a retrieval system, or transmitted by any means without the written permission of the author.

First published by CrossBooks 11/2/2010

ISBN: 978-1-6150-7264-4 (sc)

Library of Congress Control Number: 2010908266

Printed in the United States of America
Bloomington, Indiana

This book is printed on acid-free paper.

I've never seen my mother's face, but I've touched it.
I've never seen a babbling brook, but I've heard it.
I've never seen a cake rise hot and brown in the oven, but I've smelled it.
I've never seen a tomato grow in the garden, red and round, but I've tasted it.
I don't have to see God to know Him,
Since "faith comes by hearing, and hearing by the word of God."

Margie Hinkle

Prologue

It has all been wonderful. If there's ever any fussing or growling around here, it's me who does it. When Billy gets tired of hearing me growl about something, he just says, "Margie." And I hush. David is married and has two sons, Joseph and Daniel. I have pictures, and everyone says they are gorgeous. Billy has two grandchildren, Amanda and Matthew. His son Tim died in 2005. We go to a wonderfully loving church and have made many friends there as a couple. About a dozen of my blind friends that I went to school with have homes here in the Villa Maria. My sister Jody has her own apartment in Knoxville with caregivers around the clock. Judy has two boys, Sam and Howard. God has given me some beautiful things lately to fill my mind with, and that is the best thing that could happen to me. One has been writing my life story. Thank you for letting me share it with you. There are so many things I didn't get to share. Just let me say, God has brought many people into my life to help me along the way. Dr. Fry is one of the many whom I will never forget. She told me that every healthy person should have a goal to reach for, or else your life will not progress emotionally healthy. Reverend Millard White helped me to make my third album and took me to many, many churches to sing. It was fun. And, in spite of having a total of 76 breaks and fractures throughout my life, I am able to attend church regularly and do many of the things I have always enjoyed.

My Billy and I love each other dearly, that's really wonderful. I had two marriages that were not healthy. And, through the power of prayer and faith in God and family, I have reconciled with my son, which has been such a blessing to me.

I want my story to be about how God got me to this point. I'm where I am in my life now because God got me here, and I couldn't have done it by myself. I want to tell about all the things I prayed for. I want to build the story on all the things God did for me throughout my life because He got me here. I am telling the stories.

Introduction

When I was a baby, my mother dedicated me to God. At the age of three and a half, I gave my heart and life to the Lord Jesus. From ages nine to twelve I had to drop out of school because I was unable to walk.

I am now married to Billy Hinkle. My son is now grown and has two babes of his own. I was privileged when God brought a little blind girl, Kelly, into my life who became my "heart child". Kelly is grown now, too, and doing well. I also believe my sister, Jody, has played a big role in my life.

Although I have never been able to see, through faith I can see the beauty of God's handiwork and know the value of serving Him. I believe I have a great story to tell, and in this book, I will be telling my story.

Chapter 1

I was born in Newport, Tennessee, on May 2, 1940, to Tinsley Burnett and Elma Rector Clevenger. I was born with a bone condition known as osteogenesis imperfecta militis. My bones were so fragile, they were referred to in those days as "chalk bones". Also, my eyes had stopped developing after seven months in the womb. So, I was born blind and very tiny.

My mom lived in the country, on the Strawplains Pike near Knoxville, when she met my daddy, who lived in Newport. Daddy was a rambunctious kind of guy. When they first met, Mama was going with a nice guy named Gilbert. Once, when Daddy saw them together, he got so mad that he jumped in his car, sped off and squealed the tires. Mama thought, "He must love me if he got that mad," so she started going with my daddy, but she always wondered what it would have been like if she had stayed with Gilbert. Mom and Dad married shortly after she graduated from high school.

In 1938, a baby girl named Emma Joann was born, who came to be called little Jody. She was so tiny they could set her in a teacup. The baby turned blue her first night, and they thought that she wasn't going to make it. Mama asked everyone to pray for her. Even the doctors didn't think that she would make it past a year old. Mama had a baby buggy fixed for Jody, and she would get up and check on her in the night to make sure that she was still breathing. Jody wouldn't eat, and she developed rickets. When they would rattle things in front of her, she wouldn't reach for them, and that's when they found out that she was blind. The soft spot on Jody's head was only the size of a marble; it should have been the size of an egg. Because it was so small, it closed up much faster than it should have and didn't allow her brain to grow like it should. Years later, when they took me to Vanderbilt for my diagnosis, they took Jody, also, and it was discovered that she, too, had osteogenesis imperfecta militis. OIM is now called the glass bone syndrome, meaning that the bones are so brittle they break like glass. Another recessive gene which became dominant was passed down, and this gene caused us to be blind.

Eighteen months after Jody was born, Mama gave birth to another baby girl that was me, Margie. Mama sometimes had awful feelings and didn't know if she could make it through life raising two blind girls. When mom was in high school, she took an English class at some point, and they asked her to think of the worst handicap that she could imagine, and then write about it. She wrote about the handicap of blindness

After I was born, Mama decided not to have any more babies because she worried that something would be wrong with them. At first, they weren't sure that anything was wrong with me, but they must have suspected something. Mamaw Hughes, who was a good friend of my Daddy's and who taught us to call her "Mamaw", went with Mama to Vanderbilt Hospital when Jody and I were diagnosed with osteogenesis imperfecta. It was after that diagnosis that Mama had surgery so that she could not have any more babies.

When Mama was a young 21, she felt that God might be punishing her for some reason. She had no idea what He would be punishing her for. She just knew that it was a terrible thing to have two little babies who were both handicapped. *To be blind would be so awful*, she thought. *My babies will never see the birds or the flowers, the beautiful sunrise and sunset. Maybe they will never even walk. Oh, what have I done to bring two little babies like this into the world? How will I ever make it?* One day we were both crying, and Mom picked up both up, one in each arm. She pushed open the screen door and walked out to the open well. *Maybe, maybe I could throw them in and then jump, but what if I drop them in and then couldn't jump in myself? Maybe I will put them back in the baby bed and just jump in myself. Maybe I could hold them in my arms and dive in headfirst so that we would all be gone.* That kind of feeling is now called depression, deep depression. Nobody but the Doctor Above – God – could have brought her out of this depression. Daddy used the bottle to help himself get through the hard times; Mama went to the Church of God at Carson Springs.

One day soon after that, Grandma Clevenger came down. I was four or five months old. Grandma Clevenger visited with us and talked to Mama about her taking Jody to keep and see if she could get her to eat. Grandma Clevenger lived in Newport, too, just down the road from us. The help from Grandma Clevenger must have given Mama some new incentive. I'm so glad my life wasn't altered by Mom's depression. Mom was a very good mother, and the preschool training that she gave me was later said to be the best received by any student when I enrolled at the Tennessee School for the Blind.

When I was about one year old, Mama decided to have my picture made. She always loved pictures and wanted to have every memory documented in pictures. She took me to a studio and when the man tried to take my picture, all he could see through his camera was the top of my head. Little blind children, especially those who are completely blind, hold their heads down. I found out recently that there is a reason for this: Blind children can hear the sounds bouncing off the ground below them better if they keep their heads down. The man said, "I can't take her picture; all I can see is the top of her head, and you would be disappointed." Mama was hurt and a little angry, too. She took me home with the decision in mind that she would teach me to hold up my head. After that, each time she would walk through the room, she would take hold of my hair and pull up my head. Pretty soon, when I would hear her coming, I would hold up my head myself. I am glad she did that. Soon we returned to the photography studio, and this time, the photographer was able to see my face through his lens!

When I was a baby, they thought that I was not blind because when my parents shook my rattle in front of my face, I would reach for it. Mama probably knew that I was blind, but even until I was three or four years old, my aunts and uncles did not believe it. We had moved to Knoxville when I was about three years old. One day my family was visiting Aunt Lillian and Uncle Freeman, and my uncle told me that he was going to see about a horse. I said, "I want to see it!", but what I meant was that I wanted to touch the horse. My uncle told me, "Here is the horse," but he stood in front of his son, Jerry. I reached out to touch it, thinking that I would be touching a horse. When I touched it, I said, "That horse has on clothes!" I realized that it was a "people", not a horse. It was then that my uncle believed that I was, in fact, blind. My uncle then asked me if I wanted to see a chicken, and I told him, "I have to touch it to see it."

Chapter 2

Some time later, my Aunt Dorothy came to live with us while her husband Cliff was at war. One day, Mama was going to church and went to catch the bus. Aunt Dorothy was rocking baby Joyce, her daughter, in the rocking chair. I was sitting in a porch swing with Ethel Fay, the little girl who lived across the street. I said, "Ethel Fay, I want out!", and I jumped out of the porch swing -- crash. They had to call the ambulance to come, and as I started off to the hospital I told Aunt Dorothy I wanted to bring home a baby just like she had. Everyone hollered with laughter. When we got to the hospital they found that my arm and leg were broken. The doctor did not set my tibia, and it healed crooked. When it was time to come home, Mama got me a teddy bear to bring home, instead of a baby!

When I was three years old, Daddy would come home late, and my mom would hold me in her lap and rock me. Mama was my Sunday school teacher then. While she would rock me, she would tell me the Bible stories we were going to have on Sunday. She told me all about Moses and Daniel and David, and she told me about Jesus. I wished at that time that I could know Jesus like Mama did, but she said that I needed to wait until I was a little bigger. So even though I already had Jesus in my heart, I didn't make a public profession of faith until I was thirteen, because I wanted to be able to walk down the aisle like everybody else did to tell everyone that I wanted Jesus to come into my heart. In the First Baptist Church of Donelson, Preacher Baker baptized me, and I have known for sure that I'm a Christian and that I'm God's child ever since then.

Back then, we didn't have malls, so you just said you were going to town. When I was about four years old, Mom took me uptown, bought whatever she was going to buy, and then it was time to catch the bus home. She was standing in front of a store that had a really big heavy door. She was holding me in her arms because I was too tired to stand up. Even though I was four years old, I was a little bitty thing. I had my arm around her neck, and I was feeling to see what it was that we were standing against and what it felt like. I stuck my finger in this crack, and the door came to on my finger. I started crying, "Oh, Mommy, Mommy, my finger's in the door!" Some people came, but Mama couldn't turn around to get my finger out because I had my arm around her and my finger was in the closed door. Somebody finally opened the door, and I got my finger out.

Someone said, "You better rush her to the hospital." I said, "No, no, I'm not going to the hospital. I'm going home, 'cause God's going to make it well." Mama said that those people looked at her funny like they were wondering, "What are you teaching this kid?"

From when I was about three until I was nine we went to the First Assembly of God, which is a Pentecostal church. The church talked about healing more than we do in the Baptist church. I knew that God could heal.

About that time Mama said, "Here comes our bus," and we got on the bus and went home. My finger was really swollen, but she told Daddy about it that night and said that I wanted to wait until the next morning because God was going to make it well. If it was well in the morning, then she wouldn't take me to the doctor, but if it wasn't, then she would. She thought it would be well by morning. Daddy said, "Okay," because, like us, his family was Pentecostal and believed that God could heal. My finger really did get well.

Then there was another time that Mama took me uptown. You used to have to go uptown to pay the bills. You couldn't have them automatically withdrawn, and you could have sent them in the mail, but you didn't have many places to go and wanted to get out of the house. About once a week Mama would go uptown, and we would get to go into Kress's where you could buy something for twenty cents. The Krystal was across the street, and you could eat a hamburger for twelve cents. A Coke was a dime, and fries were a dime. So we would get two hamburgers, fries, and a Coke. That day while we were sitting at the Krystal, Mama said, "Oh my goodness! I've only got a five dollar bill." She asked the waitress, "Reckon you could change this?"

"Oh, honey, I'm afraid I can't change a five."

I had just been learning about how you change a one dollar bill, and I knew that two fifty cents was a dollar because fifty cents was half a dollar. So I was remembering what I had been learning, and I said, "I can!" I grabbed the five-dollar bill out of Mama's hand and tore it right in two down the middle. Mama said, "Margie, why'd you do that?"

"You've got two halves. Now it's changed." I guess Mama felt like giving me a spanking, but she didn't, because she knew that I really thought I was helping out. The girl in the Krystal had some tape, and they taped the five-dollar bill back together.

On Woodbine Avenue in Knoxville, we lived next door to Standard Knitting Mill. Daddy put up a fence down the front of the yard to keep me out of the street. However, I loved going over to visit my neighbor who gave me cookies. On the pretty days, I would crawl through the hole in the hedge and knock on Mrs. Naramore's door. One day Daddy saw me in the other yard, and he came over and got me. He put me on a stool and took his belt out of the loops on his pants. He held the belt in front of me and said, "Do you see it?" I yelled, "I don't like it!" Then I grabbed the belt from his hand and threw it across the room. Daddy went and got the belt and slapped me across the legs with it -- one smack. I cried, and he picked me up and carried me to the drug store and got me an ice cream cone. He told me never to slip through the hedge again, and if I did, he would spank me again.

During the daytime, before I went to school, Mama was busy doing the house and all that, and I made up characters to play with. Most kids have a character to play with, but you know me -- I had to have a bunch. I had Salty, Sodey, Dong-dong, Doe-doe, Pepper, and Gigi. And all of them were men, except Gigi, who was a girl. I don't know if that was because Daddy brought guys home with him sometimes to work on cars outside or what. When I started to school, Mama said, "You can't play with Salty and Sodey and Dong-dong and Doe-doe and Pepper and Gigi anymore because they'll think you're funny. You aren't supposed to play with people who aren't really there, so you can't play with them anymore." Mom said I had a funeral, and didn't play with them anymore. Oh, well, I guess I didn't need them that much after all.

Daddy would play with me when he came home at five o'clock. We would have a good evening all together, our family would, but if he came home later, then he would be drinking, and so I would go in my bedroom and play with my dolls and let Mom handle Daddy. I didn't like for him to hug and kiss me when he was drinking because I thought he smelled yucky.

Mom took me to church with her every Sunday. One Sunday as we sat in church, I was squirming around and she let me off her lap to stand beside her in the pews. My hands were always reaching to see what was around me. That morning, I felt some soft fur and said, "Kitty?" Mom lifted me up again and gave me a cracker. I was excited to see a kitty at church. "Mommy, I want to see the kitty." "Shhh, Margie, be quiet." But I just couldn't. I reached out to touch the fur again. I guess the owner of the fur coat didn't really want a little blind girl touching her coat. Mom whispered in my ear, "Margie, that's not a kitty – it's a coat!"

Chapter 3

The summer before I started school, Mama went shopping for me some clothes to wear to school. At age six, I wore size three toddler clothes. Mama bought me a dozen dresses for school.

Mama and I took a bus from Knoxville to the School for the Blind in Nashville. When meeting with the people at the school, they did not realize that it was me who would be attending the school. They said, "I thought she was too little for school."

When Mama left me at the school to go back home, she told me, "If you don't cry, I won't cry." I was playing on the swing, and Mama asked me if I was going to cry. I said, "Nope." I just kept swinging, and I didn't cry.

I was able to dress myself, which the housemother was surprised to hear. When I was little, and Mama would put on my clothes before I started school, she'd say, "I'm going to get your pretty white socks with the pretty pink lace around them to go with your pretty pink dress. You sit right here." She would get them and say, "See if you can put them on." And she would help me by telling me things like "Dresses button in the back and they have a tag in the back," so I would know back and front. She really taught me. Mrs. Anderson, my first housemother, said that I was the best pre-trained child that she had had come in, and so that made my mom feel good, because she felt like she had taught me the things I needed to know, and she had.

The very first day I was there, after Mama had left, one of the little girls, Polly, saw a doll of mine, and she cried and cried that she wanted one like it, because my doll had shoes on. I felt badly and gave the doll to the little girl. She went to sleep holding the doll, but when the teachers saw it, they took the doll away from her because they knew that it was my doll. The little girl cried again.

For school, Mama had bought me ski pajamas that were all in one piece. My roommate, Amy, and I tried and tried to get those pajamas on me that first night, but we ended up having to call for help

The next morning I went down for breakfast, and they were serving scrambled eggs. To this day, I do not like scrambled eggs. I asked for a hard boiled egg, and the teacher angrily said, "We do not have time to fix every child the kind of egg they like. You will eat scrambled or do without." I started crying and continued to cry. Finally, the teacher asked me why I was crying, and I said, "'Cause you hateful." Later, at another time, that same teacher told me that she would shake me until my teeth rattled.

On Sunday, they told everyone that they had to get ready for Sunday school, so I went back to my room to brush my hair. Mrs. Anderson then told me that I wasn't going because it was too far to walk. I got in the closet and kicked my feet up and said, "I hate you! I hate everybody, because they're going to make me go to hell!"

Mrs. Anderson told the superintendent about my tantrum, and she pulled me out of the closet and sat me in a chair and made me sit there for the three hours while the others were going to church. After a while, I fell asleep. The next Sunday, Mr. Carroll carried me all the way to the Methodist church, because I was too little to walk that far.

All the kids at school liked me, and I liked them. At first, I was afraid to go out of my room, so I got in my closet and sat on top of my trunk. One day, I crept out of the door towards the sound of the kids. The maid saw me and told me that she would lead me to the kids. I never stayed in my closet again. I always played outside with the other kids.

At that time, the administration at T.S.B. thought that children needed six weeks away from their parent to adjust. Now, they tell them to come back the next evening, so they'll know you hadn't vanished out of their life – oh, well. It had been six weeks since I had seen my mom. One night, I decided that I had better pray about this thing. "Dear Jesus, please bring my Mama to see me because I miss her a real lot, and I'm getting scared, because I haven't seen her in a long time, and I need to know if my mom is okay, and I need her to come and see me. So, please, Lord, have my mom sitting beside me in the morning. I've just got to have her. Please hear my prayer."

Mama was sitting at home that very night, and she thought, *I just can't stand it any longer. If it lacks a day or two being six weeks, then I can't help it. I'm going to Nashville, and I am going to see my baby.* She got up, packed a little overnight bag, and told my daddy to take her to the bus station, because she was going to see me. She rode the bus down to Nashville and got a cab out to the school. Mrs. Anderson came to the door and let her in, but I didn't know it. When I woke up, there she was sitting by my bed in my chair. I really knew that God had answered that prayer. God has answered prayers for me all through my life.

Chapter 4

In class, we were taught Braille. The Braille alphabet is composed of various arrangements of six dots. The teacher worked with the students one at a time teaching us Braille. I had trouble remembering my letter O, and once while working with me, my teacher, Miss Ruth Hall, pinched me on the arm. I shouted, "Ouch, you hurt me!" The teacher said, "You weren't supposed to say ouch, you were supposed to say 'Oh.'" She held me on her lap and petted me because she didn't mean to hurt me. When Miss Hall would take us one at a time, the rest of the students stayed in the library with the dorm mother, Mrs. Anderson. She taught us to sing hymns, and I loved to sing. Mrs. Anderson taught us many old, familiar hymns. I knew some of them because I had been singing in church since I was three years old. I was excited about learning those songs. Mama always told me I did well when I learned something, and when Mrs. Anderson didn't say, "Margie, you did well," I said, "Oh, Mrs. Anderson, I know all the words. What would this school do without me?" Boy, she did not like that! She said, "Young lady, this school did fine without you before you came, and it will be fine without you after you leave." I truly wondered what I had done that was so bad.

The teachers wouldn't always let me go outside even though my mother said that I could. They were afraid that I would get my bones broken. One day I was walking across the playground behind the seesaw, and it came down and hit me in the head. "It's me! Don't seesaw anymore!" I shouted. The next morning, I was shaking all over, coughing, and also had a fever. One of my friends told Mrs. Anderson. I thought that I probably had a fractured skull, but I didn't tell anyone because I didn't want to have to stay inside. All I could eat was crushed ice and orange juice. It took me about a week to get over it, and I still have a knot on my head to this day.

My family lived in the house on Woodbine in Knoxville until September of my sixth year when Mama took me to school. Then Mama and Daddy lived with Aunt Cleo through the winter while Uncle Jud and Daddy built our house in the country on a three acre lot on Osborne Road, where my mom lived until she died in 2008. Mom brought me home to an almost finished house for the summer after my first year of school. Aunt Cleo's house was right up the road, so we all stayed together quite a bit. On washdays we would all be up there together. The road was named after my mother's mother's daddy, and all the people who lived on the street were kin to each other. All the mothers and brothers were daughters and sons -- the family.

During that summer of my eighth year, Mama was making my clothes for me to go back to school in August, and I was playing "May I." I took four big steps and stepped off the rug. My foot slipped on the hardwood floor, and I fell and broke my leg and arm. At the hospital, they put both legs in the air in traction. I had to stay in the hospital for five weeks, and Mama stayed by my side night and day.

One day someone told Mama about Laverne, who ran the concession stand at the hospital. Mama went down to see Laverne to tell her about me, and then Laverne came up to see me. Laverne said, "I will get you something." "I want a Blue Bird, a little record player," I said. She brought me stories for children on record, *Little Willie and the Band*. It was a big, long 33 1/3 album. I loved that, and I would listen to it for an hour every day during naptime. I screamed if I couldn't have my records. One day when I was fussing about my records, I got a "Get Well" card from a friend. It had a poem on it that said, "There was a little girl who had a little curl right in the middle of her forehead. When she was good, she was very, very good, and when she was mean, she was horrid." "I'm not going to be mean anymore," I said. I meant it, and I wasn't mean anymore. I didn't want to be that word *horrid*.

It was during that visit that a nurse wanted to give me a shot, but I wouldn't let her. Mom said, "What is that for?" When the nurse went to look, she saw that it was the wrong shot for me. It was supposed to be given to a baby in the next room

I stayed home until Christmas, and did my second grade in one semester. I came home for the summer again and went back to school in September to start the third grade.

Back at school, November of my third grade year, we were playing "Bull in the Ring" in the gym for Phys. Ed. class. Ms. Davis was our teacher. The children stood in a circle all holding hands and I was the smallest. A bull was in the middle and was supposed to ram through the held hands in the circle. I told the boy next to me to be certain to let go of my hand if the bull came at us, but when Horace, the bull, ran at me, he hit me and my leg was broken. I was carried upstairs with my leg swinging loosely. They put a cast on me, and I had to take my lessons in the infirmary. Mom came at Christmas and brought me back in January. Then, that spring, I was sitting in the rocking chair talking to the kids, but when the nurse Marian Melvin put me back in the bed, the other leg was turned, and it broke. Now I had two broken legs, and the school called my Mama to come and get me once again

This time, I stayed at home for three years. I scooted everywhere with a pair of shoes on my hands and pair of shoes on my feet. Aunt Cleo told Mama, "She's gonna have the biggest boobs in the world!" By this time, my daddy was working at a garage in Knoxville, and some nights he did not come home until one in the morning. Those nights were scary. Also, Jody had come back home to live with our family, because Grandma Clevenger had died.

The first summer after I came home with both legs broken, Mom and I were at Aunt Cleo's, and Aunt Dorothy would come on washday, and we'd eat homemade soup for dinner. Everyone talked at the same time, but they all knew what each other said. I don't know how they did it, but they did it. One evening, Mom and Cleo were still working on their washing. Joyce was seven, Charlotte was five, and I was ten, still just wearing a size 6X dress. We were going to Aunt Dorothy's, and I told the girls, "You could pull me on a blanket." So I sat on the baby blanket (I don't know why I didn't scoot), and the girls were pulling me on the blanket. They were worried that they would have to pick me up over the mud puddle. They picked me up to lift me over the mud puddle, and they dropped me in. We all had a big laugh, and I put Charlotte's shoes on my hands and scooted all the way back to Aunt Dorothy's. There was just a little driveway between the two houses, so it wasn't very far. Mom and Aunt Cleo came in after they finished hanging out the clothes. Mom almost had a panic attack because I was gone. They knew Charlotte and Joyce would be at Aunt Dorothy's, because they went back and forth several times a day. Mama said, "How could Margie get there?" She ran out to see for sure, and there I sat on Aunt Dorothy's couch.

One time the girls hid, and Aunt Dorothy was crying, so I told her that they were hiding under the porch where I was playing with my dolls. The girls didn't like that much. They said I told on them. They would put a big tub in the yard and have the kids play and wash in the big tubs. "Keep your panties on," Mom would say to the girls. All the little boys and girls would take their baths in the tubs in the summer. It was wonderful fun. We were brown as little ginger cakes. After the water was poured out of the tub, Charlotte would get in the tub and wad up and say, "Push me down the hill, Margie," and down the hill she would go rolling, rolling, rolling.

"Now it's my turn," said Joyce Ellen.

About the time I got in the tub, Mom ran out and said, "No, no, no, she'll be broke to pieces!" That was one ride I missed.

Chapter 5

During those three years at home, Mom moved us all to town. We had two big rooms in the house: a big kitchen and another room that was the living room. A big square wooden radio sat behind the door. I would sit on that radio everyday and listen to *Pepper Young's Family*. It was a soap opera about a little girl named Edith, but they called her "Dith." That was how she said her name because she was just a baby. The story was that Linda kidnapped Dith because she had kept her for a long time while Andy and Edie were away. When they came back, Linda didn't want to let them have the little girl back, so she ran away with her. It was a good story. Jody and I slept on a couch that made a bed, in the room across from Mom and Daddy's bed. Mama made it look real pretty, just like every house we lived in. Mom got a wheelchair from somewhere while we lived there, and she would push Jody and me down to the ice cream store. We sure liked that. Daddy was a welder, and he made me a swing. Mama said it wasn't pretty, so he painted it. Even Jody would sit in the swing sometimes. There was also a porch swing there, and Jody loved me to swing her in it.

I could have cared less whether we lived in the country or in town. One reason we had moved to town was so that we could get a home teacher to come out. His name was Mr. Wallace, and if we lived in town he would be able to teach me. Mom would meet him at the bus stop, and then we would eat dinner, and then he would teach me, and then it was time for the bus. He didn't get much teaching in, because we spent most of the time eating dinner.

That year, Daddy wanted to take me to the fair because I had never been. Daddy was going to take me and Mary Ellen Walker, the little girl who lived next door. Of course, Mom went, too. I don't know why they didn't get a wheelchair for me, but they didn't, so Daddy carried me a long way, all the way to the carousel. We stepped on and saw that all the horses were full. One little boy said that I could ride with him, but I didn't know the little boy, so I was bashful, and I was scared I might fall, too. Daddy said we'd ride the next time. As Daddy started to get off the carousel, his foot got caught in a cable, and he tripped. Over in a flip we went, and Daddy's hip landed on my ankle. Oh, did it swell! We were sitting there on the ground, and I was crying. Mama said, "Well, T," (that's what they called my daddy), "let's just go back home."

So Daddy got up and lifted me back in his arms. We got back to our car, and I was still crying. A guy asked, "What happened, T?"

Daddy said, "Oh, my baby has brittle bones, and I wanted to bring her to the fair. She can't walk, so I carried her, and clumsy me, I fell, so we are going to go back home."

"Who was that, Daddy?" I asked. He answered, "It was a policeman. He is a friend of mine."

We went back home, and my foot was swollen really big. Mom said that she guessed they had better head to the hospital. I cried my heart out, "Please, Mommy, please! Don't make me go there again." We thought this was the ninth broken bone. Mary Ellen's mother told Mom to soak a brown paper bag in vinegar water, put it around my foot, then wrap a towel around it, and see if it didn't take the swelling down. By the next afternoon, the swelling was down, and I was scooting around using two hands and one foot. I even scooted out to my swing and swung some. So Mom decided not to take me to the hospital.

After that we moved back out to the country. We were glad to get back into our home. The first summer I came home to the country, my legs weren't hurt anymore, but they weren't strong. I still couldn't walk, but I went to Bible School, and Ms. Odem, who was a big woman, would carry me up and down the stairs. She probably had a backache for weeks after that! I still wore a child's size six in a dress then. They asked me to sing a solo at Bible school that year.

As busy as I was, and as busy as I kept my parents, my sister, Jody, was always sure to get her share of the attention, too. I was always close to Jody, and when I came home from school, I would sing to Jody and teach her poems. Jody loved me, and she always liked to play with me. Jody could not walk. I now believe that Jody was autistic, and certainly not mentally retarded. Jody's head was hurt at birth because of the osteogenesis, and she is deaf in one ear. The little skulls of babies with osteogenesis are very brittle and fragile, and the doctors sometimes fracture the skull as the babies are being born.

Jody didn't like dolls but Mama had an old doll that her brother brought her from the war. I wouldn't have let anyone touch that doll if I were her. It was a baby doll, and Jody found it one day while she was just crawling around. Whatever she found she would play with. Jody got the doll, and as she was holding it, I asked her, "What's its name?" She replied, "Knowledge Town." One day, she got that doll and started hitting its head on the ground. She said she was going to hurt Knowledge Town. I don't know why she got so mad. I shouted, "Mommy, come quick! Jody's beating Knowledge Town in the head." Mama didn't come, and Jody beat Knowledge Town until it broke.

Jody wanted a "cookie doll" so she could sit in its lap. That was a big rag doll with long legs. Mama made Jody and me both one for Christmas. On Christmas morning, Mom had our little breakfast table and the two dolls sitting in the chairs in our room. Jody also wanted a football named Teensy and a wagon she could sit in. I cried because I thought Santa Claus wouldn't know if I had a brother or a sister.

Jody has a funny way of naming things and people. She called the hospital "hostittle," and when I got married, Jody called my husband Billy Hinkle "little Tillie Winkle." When she was little, she named a puppy Gardenia. I had a doggy, and she had puppies. I asked her, "Jody, do you want this to be your puppy so Mom will let you keep it?" She said, "I want that little puppy, Gardenia." Jody called Mama her "little Elma Mama." Later, at Green Valley and Cloverbottom, where they moved Jody when she got older, they call all the nurses "Mama-this" and "Mama-that." Jody calls me her "little sis-tah Mah-gie." She bends one arm and puts it up in the air when she wants me to hug her.

She sometimes had tantrums, and Mama would respond by carrying her around. The doctor told Mama to put Jody in a room by herself when she threw her tantrums. Mama did just that, and after a while, Jody got quiet. When she opened the door, Mama found that she had torn the ruffle off of the chair and was tearing up the curtains, and that was the end of that.

When she was little, Jody refused to eat, which is why Grandma Clevenger insisted on keeping her. Some days she had nothing but coffee and milk. But, as Jody got older, she learned to eat better. Today, Jody is only thirty-six inches tall and fifty pounds. Mama would often ask me to play with Jody. I knew that I could make Jody happy.

With the two girls at home, Mama had it difficult getting any time out of the house. She crocheted lots of things for Jody and me. In the winter, she crocheted clothes for the Little Red Riding Hood doll and a wedding party with a bride and groom and a bunch of bridesmaids storybook dolls for me. The doll clothes were starched real stiff. I loved dolls and had lots of pretty ones. I had a child's table and chairs and a set of dishes, and I played house all day long. I learned to cry like a baby, and I made a different voice for each doll. An insurance man came to the house one day while I was playing, and he asked Mama if all of those children were hers. She replied that it was only one child playing: Margie.

Chapter 6

I stayed home for three years at that time when I had to come home in March. I wanted to go back to school really, really badly. All the other kids were going back to school, and I was so lonesome. I was twelve years old, and one night I told my Mama that I was going to pray that God would heal my legs so that I could go back to school. I began to pray that God would heal my legs so that I would be strong enough to go back to school. I went to bed that night, and it was in the wintertime and really cold. We had just a heater in the living room. I slid out from under my good warm covers, and I knelt down on my knees, and I put my head on the bed and I started to pray. I said, "Dear Jesus, I don't mind being blind. I really don't, but I mind being too short. So the thing I'm going to pray about is my legs. God, I've had a lot of broken legs, but they have always healed in the past. I just got over one, and I got the other one broke, and neither one is strong enough for me to stand on. God, I don't mind being blind, but can't You just please heal my legs and let me go back to school?" So I'm sitting there, and I'm praying, and all of a sudden it hit me: *God doesn't have to do what you want Him to do. You're talking ugly to the Lord. You're telling Him what you think He ought to do.* So I started praying, "Lord, if you let me walk again, I promise you that I will use my legs for the glory of God. I will do anything you want me to. If someone says, 'Come and sing,' or, 'Come and give your testimony,' I'll go, Lord, so please let me walk again for Your glory." Then I asked in Jesus' name and got back into bed, and I knew I would walk again. I thought, *I really think I'm going back to school. I really believe God is going to let me walk because I'm going to use my legs for His glory.*

The next morning I got out of bed and scooted in the kitchen and got up in my chair. I said, "Mom, you better get busy making my dresses. I'm going back to school next year." She said, "You are?" "Yep," I answered. She said, "When do you think you're going?" I said, "Oh, I guess I'll go right after Christmas." She said, "Alright."

So Mama went to town and started getting material and making my dresses, which were size 9. Every day I kept trying to stand up, but I couldn't stand up yet. I had braces I was supposed to be wearing, so I put on my braces, and I was able to stand up. I was able to walk through the house holding on to things. I could feel the strength growing in my legs. The Knoxville News Sentinel came out and wrote my story about how I wanted to go back to school. They wrote that I was wearing my braces and they thought that the School for the Blind ought to let me come back because I wanted to come. No one else at school had any other handicap except being blind. Mr. Stevens, the school superintendent, came out to see me. He asked me if I would wear my braces if I came back to school, and I said I would. I wanted a wheelchair, so we got a big old rickety thing from the Red Cross. I was scared of it because it shook when they put me in it. My little cousin Charlotte went home and emptied her piggy bank, and Aunt Cleo asked her why she was emptying her bank. She said, "I have to buy Margie a wheelchair. She don't like the one the Red Cross sent her because she is afraid it might fall." Charlotte must have been about seven at the time. Aunt Cleo thought that was the neatest thing that Charlotte wanted to buy me a wheelchair. I don't know exactly how they did it, but everybody wanted to help buy me a wheelchair, so they took up a collection and bought me a pretty little wooden wheelchair. Mr. Stevens said I could bring it back to school with me, and my mom could pay two little girls to push me back and forth from the dorm to meals and to class and back. Those little girls could room with me and help me. Mama asked how much she would have to send them. He said three dollars a week for each girl, which would be six dollars a week, which would be twenty-four dollars a month. Mom thought that was all she could afford. That was a lot of money back then.

After Christmas, Uncle Alfred and Aunt Cleo and Mom took me to school, and I went into the third grade. The housemother didn't much want me to come, and she took Mama and showed her all the places I might get hurt. She said, "Here's the rec room, and she might fall right down those stairs." "I won't, Mama. I'll know they're there, and I won't fall down them," I said. I would remember them forever since the housemother threw such a fit. They put me in one of the two dorm rooms downstairs. Marie and Amy were going to be the girls to take care of me. They were both sweet little girls, and I had roomed with Amy when I was little, about six. Amy and I were the ones who had trouble getting my pajamas on. Amy and Marie were real glad to room with me. They would put me in my wheelchair and back me down the steps and push me to breakfast. They would leave the wheelchair outside because it was hard for them to get it inside and back out. They would leave it at the foot of the steps. When we came back, I would hold on to them real tight, and they would help me down the steps, and I would get in the wheelchair. Then they would get me up the stairs in the dorm and take the wheelchair inside, but at the school building they left it outside. Then I would hold onto their arms and walk down the hall to my class. My teacher that term was Mrs. Nichols, and I really liked her.

I could walk pretty well in my braces. I knew my legs were getting stronger, and I knew that God was going to make them stronger. Mrs. Nichols asked me if I would walk back and forth across the hall with a girl who was having trouble walking. Everyday Ann Carol and I would walk across the hall and back, and we would do that all dinner hour. That was good for me and her both, and so one day I said, "Let's race!" So we held hands and we raced. One day she ran off and left me. She had gotten strong enough that she could run off and leave me, whereas I had been the strongest in the beginning. Now she could walk well enough to go outside and play with the kids and stuff, I told Mrs. Nichols that I was tired of doing walking with her.

Mrs. Nichols only did something one time that made me not like and respect her the way I had all the time I had known her. Mrs. Nichols was going to walk with me outside, and she said, "I'm going to see how far you can walk by yourself."

I said, "Okay, but you have to tell me if there are any steps."

She said, "Okay," and we walked that day and everything was fine. So the next day we walked, and she stepped down off the curb and let me just come to the step and fall against her.

I said, "I won't ever trust you again. Not ever!"

She said, "I just wanted to see what would happen if you did come to a step."

"I would fall just like I told you," I said. "I won't ever trust you again." And she told me she was sorry and would not do it again. She was real sweet to me for the rest of the year, but I never trusted her again. That was the end of that story.

Chapter 7

I wanted to take piano lessons at school, and I was so excited to get to take them. I had taken piano about six years before when I could walk, after my Aunt Lillian met Miss Hale on the bus, and they talked about me taking piano lessons. Miss Hale was blind, and she wanted to teach me, but my hands were too little, and I couldn't reach the notes. The song that I knew was "Sand Man." But in the spring of that third grade year, Mrs. Nichols took me down to Miss Lois, who was Miss Lois Bible at the time, later Mrs. Lois Cole, and now is Mrs. Lois Propst. She was young, wasn't married yet, and she was the sweetest thing. She and I talked almost all the time the first day. The next time she said, "Let's play a piece today," and she started to teach me the fingering. She gave me a little piece to start working on, and she helped me learn Braille music. One day I went in for a lesson, and she said, "Margie, I have to talk to you."

"Are you mad?" I asked.

"I don't know."

"Why are you mad?"

"You know, this is a brand new building we are in," she said. They had just finished the new school in Donelson. It used to be in Nashville across the street from the General Hospital. "You know all of these are brand new pianos and new benches. Well, someone has scratched the seat of one of our piano benches, and they have scratched it all to pieces. It's the piano room I took you to practice in. Do you know anything about this?"

"No, I would never scratch piano benches," I said. However, we soon discovered that my leg braces had done the damage. I cried, and cried, and cried. Oh, it just tore me up. I didn't mean to hurt the bench. I had no idea it was happening. My braces had a little screw in the back to hold the leather against the steel, and that little screw was hurting the bench. And oh, that just broke my heart. It just killed me.

Miss Lois said, "From now on, you will just practice in one room." That way, if I ruined a bench it would just be one bench. And so I really felt bad, and I cried half the day that day. That was one thing that the braces did. Another was that my pretty dresses, size 2 by now, would get caught in the knee joints of the braces. Little slits were cut all around the bottoms of my dresses.

I was planning to still wear my braces and have the girls push me back and forth in the wheelchair, but at the very end of my third grade year, I pulled off my braces one day. I was sitting on the bed, and I stood up to fix the bow on my dress. I moved one foot a little bit, and then I was walking. I got half way across the room, and I had to holler for help. I had no idea I could walk, and after not being able to walk for three years, this was a miracle! I had Mom come down. She knew my surprise before I showed her, so that was really great. I could walk down to take a shower and stand there and take a shower with her holding my hand without the braces.

That summer when I went home, I was trying to walk and not scoot anywhere anymore. Once in a while, I would get out of my chair at the table, and I would go scootin' through the house, and Mom would say, "Margie, how come you're scootin' again?" It was funny. I'd say, "Oh, I forgot." I would come back and get in my chair, and I would stand up and put one hand on the table, and I would walk until I felt something else I could put my hand against because I was still scared. We had a big wide archway between our living room and the dining room, and so everyday I tried to walk across the archway by myself without the braces because now I knew I could stand up okay. I would walk from one side of this big arch to the other side, and I would say, "Mama, stand close to me so I can do this." So she would stand close to me, and I did it, and did it, and did it, and finally I could do it well.

About that time Mama said, "Now, stand up straight."

And I said, "I thought I was standing up straight." I was standing there, but I was kind of bent over. I felt too tall because I was used to being on the floor. I raised up a little bit and would ask, "Is that straight?"

"No, you're still bent over. Go back there and stand next to the archway and put your back against the wall. Now straighten all the way up against the wall, and that's how you can tell if you're straight. Now walk." I would go across there and as I came, I would bend back over. One day she said, "You're still not standing up straight."

"Well, just stand me up straight then," I said. She came behind me and straightened me up, and she would hold my shoulders back while I walked. Soon I was able to walk standing straight by myself.

By the time I started back to school again, I could walk standing up straight. I went to school, and I still had my braces. I was in the fourth grade now, and in September, I went to the Junior League Hospital. My doctor was Dr. Ashby. "Well, young lady, how are you doing?" he asked.

"I'm doing great. I can stand up without my braces," I answered.

"You can?"

"I can. I want to show you."

I started untying my braces, and he said, "Wait a minute! Wait a minute here!"

"I have to take off my braces to show you."

"You have to be really careful." He and his nurse lifted me off the table and put me down very gently. Then I stood up, and he said, "Here, hold my finger," and so I did, and I walked. He said, "Oh, my Lord! Stand right here! No, sit in this chair just a minute." He went out, and he came back, and he had all the resident doctors and all the nurses that were on duty at that time. He brought them all in and said, "Now, I want all of you to stand in a circle. Make a big circle, and stand in it, and put your hands out. If she starts to fall, you are to get her. Don't let her fall." He then said to me, "Now you walk across the diameter of the circle." So I stood up, and I walked across the circle, and they all went, "Ohhhh!" He had shown them my x-ray before I walked, and my bones were no bigger around than a pencil.

Dr. Ashby then said, "We were afraid for this young lady to walk because we were afraid her bones would break, and for three years, she must have been afraid, too, because she didn't walk. And now she is walking without her braces. This is a miracle! We can't let her go out of here in the braces when she can walk without them." He got an old pair of shoes that were too little for me, and he said, "Here, we can just cut the toes out." They cut the toes out. "Now take her and buy her some new shoes," and they gave us a coupon and told us what store to go to. They said, "Go without your braces in the morning and wear them in the afternoon." When I went back, they said to keep them off all the time. I could now walk without my braces. That was wonderful. All those doctors knew that my bones were no bigger around than a pencil because they had seen my x-rays. They could see that this was really a miracle. When I was little, I had so many breaks. Every time I turned around, I was broken. All that year I grew stronger and stronger, and I didn't have any more breaks the rest of school, which added to the miracle. I was able to graduate without any more breaks, and it was really fabulous.

Chapter 8

By this time, I was thirteen years old, and I wanted to go to parties, but the junior parties were too rough and wild for me. I just had to sit back and watch all the other kids. One day, in fourth grade, Ronald Bridges came in, and he said, "Hey, I want to tell you something."

I said, "What?"

He said, "There's a guy I know, he's my friend, and he wants to go with you."

I said, "Why?"

"Well, he likes you, he likes your voice, and he wants to go with you."

"What's his name?"

"Buddy."

"Where does he want to go?"

"He wants to sit with you at recess."

I said, "Okay."

So we go out in the hall for recess, and Ronald hollers, "Hey, Townsend! Townsend! Come 'ere. She said 'Okay'."

The boy came over and said, "Hi, I'm Buddy, and I already know you're Margie. I'm in the fifth grade." I said "Oh, okay," and we started talking, and I don't know what all we talked about. As the year went on he would tell me sweet things. He said, "Oh, you're so pretty. You just look like an angel." Oh, he was romantic. We wrote notes back and forth to each other in the dorm.

Once when we were going together, Buddy and I went to this park, and there was a big bunch of bushes there. We had been there before, and it was kind of in the woods. Buddy said, "When we get off the bus, and I take your hand, you come." And Richard said, "When Margie takes Buddy's hand, Betty, you follow." The guys had planned this. Buddy and Betty were partially sighted, and Richard was going with Betty then, and I was going with Buddy. We hadn't had a chance to kiss and stuff. We were younger then, and Buddy was about to die to give me a kiss. So we got in the woods, and we sat on this log for a few minutes, and then we got up and walked further and further into the woods. Then we weren't sure what way to go to get back. Anyway, we kissed and hugged, and he told me that he was going to be a preacher when he grew up, and all this. So that was the first time we ever got to kiss, and we decided, oh yes, we really loved each other.

Soon Mr. Wood started calling, "Lunch, lunch! Everybody come to lunch! Wherever you are, come to lunch!" So we started down, following his voice, and so we got back, and he asked, "Where have y'all been?" And we said, "We've been in the woods." We were sure he'd think there couldn't have anything smoochie going on, as this was really the olden days. Like I said, we weren't even allowed to hold hands or anything.

The following week, the supervisor came up and said, "Margie, tell me about that day. What did you and Buddy do when you were in the woods? Mr. Wood is about to have a fit. He is just worried to death that one of y'all did something you weren't supposed to do, and you will end up pregnant."

"We didn't do anything like that. We just kissed. Can that make you pregnant?"

"No, I don't think so."

"We just talked, and Buddy said he was going to be a preacher," I said.

"Okay. I can tell Mr. Wood he can quit worrying about you."

Meanwhile, one of Mr. Wood's daughters got pregnant that year. His son, Jim Wood, would slip off to Donelson in the night. Here he was worrying about us, and here his kids were doing everything. It was something.

One time these boys, Butch Davis and another guy, decided they were going to run away. They weren't going to stay at school any longer. They hated it, and they were going to run away. Most of the kids didn't feel like that at all. Anyway, Butch and the other guy ran off, and Jim Wood told his father, "Hey, I saw two of the kids from school crossing the railroad track down there. Were they supposed to?"

Mr. Wood said, "Oh, no! Who was it? Who was it?" He ran off hunting them, but the boys had gotten quite far away before he got them and bought them back. They had run off about four times, and finally he sent Butch home, so we didn't have any more runaway episodes after that. They just didn't like the rules and how things were and just ran away.

Fifth grade is a year I will long remember, as my classmates became very permanent. In 5th grade, we became the class that would graduate from high school together. The five girls were Judy Munsey, Marie Parton; Linda Lunsford, Maxine Hornbuckle and me. The boys were Ralph Brewer, Clifford Wilson, Ronald Bridges, William Dorris Lane, Zeke Ward, J. T. Miller, Danny Hollis, Marion Womack, and Charlie Moore. In fifth grade I never realized I would grow up to someday marry one of the guys!

All we girls were so close. We had such a bond. We knew and felt what each other was thinking. Some mornings when we would go from the dorm to class I could walk faster than the others. When I would be poking along, Marie and Linda would say, "Come on, Margie." "I'm coming as fast as I can," I'd respond. They'd bend their elbows and say, "Hang on!" I'd reach up and grab hold and off they'd go, running as fast as they could. That is a happy time to remember. They did that so often I will never forget it, and sometimes I still dream that I'm flying! Sometimes it would be Linda and Maxine or maybe Judy once in a while. Judy and I dug a little hole by the swing set when we were in 4th grade. We pricked our wrists with a pin and put them together then wiped our blood on a little piece of cloth and buried it in the hole. We promised that from then on, no matter what happened, we would be blood sisters. Every time I think of Maxine I think of oranges, as she was always eating them. I wanted to be like her so I would save my orange from dinner, and we would go through the morning eating one orange slice at a time. Oh, did they smell good. I'd sometimes miss evening piano practice and slip off to the playroom to sit on the big couch, drinking a Coke and talking with Marie. We told each other everything. We still do the same today. I love my Linda so much, and I get hungry to see her. For my 69th birthday I asked for the gift of being together with four classmates who live here in Nashville -- Linda, Ralph, Marie and Marion. We went to Dalt's and ate them out of house and home.

We all became so close through our years together in school, and more than 50 years later, we are all still good friends. The summer after we graduated Zeke Ward passed away from cancer. We were saddened as we did not want any of the class to be gone. Then, in 2005, W. D. Lane passed away.

One really cold and snowy winter night in the fifth grade, we were all bored. Thirty of us girls from fourth to tenth grade needed to find something to do. The housemother was a relief housemother, and she was quacky, and we didn't think she knew anything. The girls said, "Margie, come here. We want you to do something. We want you to get in the laundry room and get down in the dirty sheets. When we knock on the door, we want you to cry like a baby, and when we knock again, then hush." So I got in the clothes, and they said, "Cry like a baby." I did, and they said, "Yeah, that's good," and I quit.

The girls then went upstairs and got Ms. Wontland. She came down the stairs, and the girls told her, "We hear a baby outside. Somebody has left a baby outside the dorm."

"You are full of it," she said.

"No, you just walk down the hall, and you hear it." Every time she would get away from the door, I would cry so that she wouldn't know where it was coming from. They took her outside, and when she got by the window, I would cry.

Ms. Wontland said, "They are going to have to call someone to hunt that baby. I can't find it!"

Over the summer, Buddy wrote me letters, Braille letters. Oh, Lord, it was letters like I read in books now, and he wasn't very old, you know. As a matter of fact, even though he was a grade ahead of me, I was three years older than him because I had missed three years of school. But none of the kids in my class really even thought about me being older because I was the smallest one in there. So that was, I guess, one time when my size was to my advantage. They soon grew off and left me, but because we were together then, nobody ever thought anything about it. Once my mom came to school when I was in the eighth or ninth grade. Some of the ninth and tenth graders came in with us for science, and Mama said, "Here, no, that's not the right class. You can't be in with these big ol' boys, can you?" "Mama, it's not the boys that's big, it's me that's too little!" I told her. She couldn't imagine that I was in there with all those big old boys. That was funny to think that the mom would say such a goofy thing.

Chapter 9

When we went back to school in September of my sixth grade year, we all had new crinolines to wear under our full skirts. Some of my crinolines were taffetarized, and I would starch them by dipping them in a whole box of Stayflow Starch mixed with water. We would spread them up on the tile wall, and when they dried, they rattled like paper. One day, I wore two of them with a full skirt. When the classroom was completely quiet, they would rattle when I moved. My teacher, Miss Wisdom, was blind, but she heard everything! When I moved, she said, "Alright, children, who has food in here?" Nobody said a word. Then she started reading again, and as hard as I tried, I had to move again. "Alright, I'm going to catch you," she said. She started over by the window. She was feeling in everybody's desk and in their hands. She got over to me, and Ronald Bridges said, "Miss Gerdy, that's Margie's crinoline. Nobody's got food." I thought, "Boy, I've had it. I'm going to hit that Ronald Bridges when class is over." But Miss Wisdom said in the kindest, calmest voice, "Alright, Marjorie, if you must wear the things, keep still."

Later in the year, I had bad headaches, and Buddy got appendicitis, which found us both in the school infirmary. That's when Buddy's mother met me and my Mama. Buddy's mother told Mama, "They've got to break up. I married his daddy, and I divorced him after Buddy was born handicapped because I didn't want to have any more handicapped children. I will not have him going with a handicapped girl, because certainly I'm not going to let him grow up and have handicapped children." When Mama told me that, I said, "We don't care what she thinks. We'll just go together anyway."

Buddy came to school the next year, I guess we were in seventh and eighth grade, and he said, "Margie, we can't go together anymore."

I said, "Why?"

He said, "My mom said that I couldn't." I just sat there and didn't say anything, and he said, "She said we'll look silly together when we get out of school, because I'm a big tall man, and you're a little tiny woman."

I said, "Well, if you think that, then I guess we would." Then I went to the dorm, and I cried, and cried, and cried.

After that I started going with Richard. Buddy could see a little bit, but Richard was completely blind. It just liked to have killed me when I first started going with Richard because he never did say how pretty I was and stuff like that, and he didn't give me compliments to make up for it, either. So evidently, he wasn't a complimentary person because blind boys can think of as many sweet things to say as boys that can see. But Richard didn't, and I missed that so bad. I thought, *No matter how much I fix up, or how much I fix my hair, or how much I smile, or how much I do anything, he's never going to tell me I'm pretty because he can't see me. And if he doesn't think I'm pretty, I'm not sure if I want to go with a blind boy or not. Here I am blind, but I don't know if I want to go with a blind boy or not. I'm very vain.*

Richard and I went ahead and went together, and every time Buddy would come along I would just not smile, because I wanted Buddy to see that I was still depressed because we were broken up. I was doing it on purpose for Buddy to see, because I really thought that I loved him because I was his angel and everything. One day Richard said, "Margie, I want to ask you something."

"What?"

"Will you do me one favor?"

"What?" I asked.

"If you don't smile any other time, would you please start smiling when Townsend's around? 'Cause he thinks that I'm not making you happy."

I said "Okay." I didn't want to, but I started smiling a little bit.

One day he said, "Why is it that you don't smile while Townsend's around?"

"Because I still miss him."

"Well, what do you miss?" he asked.

"Well, he was always telling me how pretty I was, and he was always saying sweet things to me."

"Well, I can do that."

"Yeah," I said, "but you don't." So Richard started telling me how pretty I could sing.

At the end of the year, we had concerts on the day we went home for the summer. That way the parents could come to get us and hear the programs at the same time. Mom got there for me about one o'clock in the afternoon. "Oh, Mom, please don't make me go yet. Please stay and hear the concert tonight."

"Margie, Daddy will have to drive all night in the dark if we stay. We are going home now. I'm sorry, but that's the way it has to be." I pouted all the way home because I was broken hearted. We were going to do this beautiful choral piece, Chopin's Etude in E Major. The tune was "O Sacred Art," a classical love song. I had been the one to ask the choral teacher to let us sing it. It was beautiful, and the choral teacher said that it wasn't the same song without me there to sing the lead soprano.

In the summer Richard and I would write letters, of course. My cousin Jerry Lee had a tape recorder, and I would walk over to Jerry and Joyce's house (it was almost a mile), and I would listen to Richard's letter on the recorder, and then I would tape him one. I would do that about once a week, and my cousin would stay in the room with me because it was special for her to hear my love letter. I had another cousin, Dixie, who lived in Chattanooga, where Richard lived. When Dixie came to visit in the summer, I begged Mama to let me go back with her. Cousin Dixie had a daughter, Linda Gail, who was three years younger than me, but as far as we were concerned, we were the same age. When her daughter Linda Gail was going on a date, Dixie would make them go over and pick up Richard so that we could double date. Oh, man, I thought we were plum normal then. We got to go double dating in a car. That was fabulous because blind kids don't get to do that. We really had a good time going to movies and just riding, pulling over somewhere to park. We just did what normal kids do.

I had a big roll of Braille letters from my sweetheart, Buddy, from the year before, a whole big stack. When I would see them in my drawer, I would just about cry. Mama said, "Why don't you just throw them away?" There was a popular song out at the time called, "Cross Over the Bridge". At the end of Mama's driveway, which was pretty long, was a little creek. There was a wooden bridge that you walked over or drove over to get to the driveway. One day, my cousin Carolyn and I went down, and we threw part of the letters off on one side and part of the letters off on the other side, and we sang "Cross Over the Bridge": *Cross over the bridge, cross over the bridge. Leave your reckless ways behind you. Cross over the bridge. Leave your fickle past behind you, and true romance will find you, brother. Cross over the bridge.* So we sang that, and by the time the letters had sunk down into the creek and we had walked over the bridge a few times, I forgot to be sad and started laughing.

Chapter 10

I got to date the year I was in the eighth grade. But, remember -- they wouldn't even let us hold hands on our dates. On Sunday afternoon, the boys and girls could be together. We would sit in a row in couches and chairs lined up all around a lounge. Each couple could sit together, but we had better not be caught holding hands, or huggin', or anything. The boys would get one of the guys who didn't have a girl to stand in the door of the room, and if somebody was coming, they would say, "Mayday, mayday!" And we would all quit kissing. I mean, if we had sat there all Sunday afternoon, it would have been abnormal if we didn't find some way to have a kiss. The school never caught on to that.

One of my favorite things was going to the high school socials, and I danced the whole time. Of course, I was really short, and I would have my hand up on Richard's shoulder and look up at him. The gym teacher said, "Margie, you're going to break your neck if you don't stop holding your head back to look at Richard. Why do you do that anyway? You can't see."

"Well, we have to hear each other," I said.

"He's going around with his head down, and you're going around with yours thrown back! Oh, my Lord!"

In that same year the wrestlers came to Tennessee to wrestle our team. Mr. Wood said that the boys could walk the girls back to the dorm because we had company. It was a treat for everybody. We had a party, a social. Everybody danced with everybody, and then the boys walked us home. When Polly heard us coming up, she turned out the lights. We all crowded on the porch, and we were kissing to beat the band. I said, "Oh Richard, I've got to go. I'm scared."

"You mean the one time that we would have a chance to really kiss, and you're scared of it?"

"Yes, I am. In my stomach, I just feel that something's wrong. I'm going in."

"Alright, do that," he said.

"Please don't be mad at me. I have to." So I went in, and I said, "Turn the lights back on, Polly."

She said, "If I hear Mrs. Beetle coming back downstairs, I will." So I went on back behind the counter, and about that time I heard Mr. Wood.

"Alright, you've hung yourselves," he said. He had slowly walked behind us all the way to the dorm. He let them all get on the porch and get really passionate, then he came behind and caught them. Oh, my Lord, I was so glad I was inside that I didn't know what to do. For the first time, I was not right in the middle of the group getting in trouble. I was so scared. *Oh, what will they do them? I hope Richard got home.*

They came in and said, "Oh, Mr. Wood has caught us."

The next day the gym teacher said, "We're not having gym today. We're having a talk. We all went in the gym room and sat down, and she said, "How many were on the porch kissing?"

Peggy, my real good friend who played Jane Eyre said, "My Mama said I could kiss Dave." Come to find out, I bet they wouldn't have known who all was kissin' if we wouldn't have told because she wouldn't have had to say, "Who all was kissing," but we were goofy.

I said, "Well, I wasn't."

"How come you wasn't?" she asked me.

"I went in."

She said, "Mr. Wood is fixing to send a group of girls to Tullahoma, to the Tennessee Preparatory School." Tullahoma was the school where they took disciplinary kids.

Peggy said, "They won't take me there. I'll call my Mama and tell her to come get me."

And I said, "I'm going to call my Mama and have her come get me, too."

The teacher said, "Well, if you weren't out there, how come you're going to call your Mama?"

"I'm scared. I'm afraid they'll just take all the girls to Tullahoma." Oh, we were scared to death. That's all we could talk about for the next week. We all wondered how come Mr. Wood hadn't said anything about it. When it was time for assembly, he got up, and he made this big speech about how this wonderful school had been made for us, and all we could think of was kissing each other, and that was ridiculous, and that wasn't part of education, and we were here for an education. "You really made a big spill," he said. So, anyway nobody was ever sent to Tullahoma, and I guess it died down.

One day we had this new dance instructor, and they wanted us to learn some new dances. So they called this little boy in who was the same height as me, who was in the third or fourth grade. Opal said, "Oh, Margie, that's Jimmy Oldham. He's just in the fourth grade!"

I replied, "And they think I'm going to dance with him?!" I started to cry, and I started having a fit, the second temper fit I had in school. But I started screaming and crying, and I said, "I am not dancing with him," and they asked why. I said, "Because he's only in the fourth grade, and I'm in high school." I was humiliated, and I knew I wasn't going to dance with Richard in any of the dance classes if I danced with Jimmy Oldham. It's funny -- now, every time I see Jim, he calls me "Princess," and he says, "Am I tall enough to dance with you now?"

I can hardly reach the top of his head. I'll say, "Hi, Jim, let's dance."

And he'll say, "Alright, princess." He has told me, "That scarred me for years. I didn't know why you didn't want to dance with me." He was so funny.

One day Peggy and I were talking. Oh, I just loved Peggy and still do. I asked her, "Well, do you ever wish that Jack could see you?" Jack was blind, too.

She said, "He has."

"What?"

"He has. I'm not going to make him not see me just because he's blind."

"What do you mean?"

"Well, I started out by letting him feel my face, and then he just kept on feeling all over me, so he's seen me. You should let Richard see you, too."

"Do you think? How would I get a chance to do that?"

"Well, when you're riding home on the bus, just put your coat over you, and let him feel of you. Oh, he would love your pretty big boobs."

I was going to Chattanooga to my cousin's house. Richard and I knew that we were going to get to go dating when I was at Dixie's house. So I rode home on the bus with him, and he put his hands under my coat to feel of me. We thought we were doing something wonderful. I thought, *Now, should I be doing this, or should I not? Peggy said that I should because Richard was blind.*

26

Richard said, "How come you let me do that? How come you let me see you? How come you let me touch your boobs?"

"I thought you should know about them since you're blind. I thought maybe you had never had a chance to feel of a girl."

"I hadn't, but how come you let me?"

"I didn't think you should stay dumb. I have a crooked leg, but you can't see it. I don't want you to see my ugly part."

So that was as far as it went, but I wanted to think that he had seen me, so he did. I told Dixie, and she said, "Well, I guess that was okay. You know since he couldn't see, and you wanted him to see what you looked like. I guess that was okay."

When I came home, I would feel so guilty like I couldn't sing in church, because I had let him touch my boobs. So I would get out my Bible, and I would read it. I was always reading in Psalms, and I would just feel more and more guilty. I would pray and ask God to forgive me, and then I could go to church and sing again. That's the way that was. Every time I did something wrong, I would have to ask God to forgive me, and I would read my Bible. Richard and I ended up going together for eight years, but he graduated two years before me. After Richard graduated, I would sometimes have a date with somebody on Sunday afternoon just because I didn't have anything else to do. I would feel lonesome because Richard was gone.

Chapter 11

The summer after eighth grade, I was at home, and it was a hard summer. I couldn't tell anymore by Daddy's actions whether he was drunk or sober, and I wondered if he was taking drugs or something. He just didn't seem like himself. He didn't seem quite alert, and he had slowness in his talk. I used to just be afraid when he was drinking, but that summer I didn't know if he was drinking or if he wasn't. I went on to school that fall, and in January, Mom told me that Daddy was sick. "Mama, if Daddy gets sicker, I want to come home. Don't keep it from me because you think I will worry." Daddy called me dumpling, sweet, and cakes. They bought me a piano, and he loved for me to sing and play the piano. He said love words to me and called me pretty. Mama said you shouldn't brag on your own child. But my confidence wasn't built because I wasn't getting any approval from Mom.

When Mama called me in February and said Daddy was sicker, she said, "I'll call you when you need to come home." One Friday at school, my friend, Judy Munsey, said, "Margie, why don't you have any books?"

"Because I'm going home. I'm going to ask Mr. Wood if he will take me to the bus station after our bowling." Before bowling was over, I heard a familiar voice. It was Edith Williams, a friend who had graduated from the school. Mom also called Laverne Humphrey, whom I met when I was eight years old and in the hospital with my broken legs. Laverne was the blind girl who worked at General Hospital.

Mama called Edith and Laverne and asked them if they would come and get me because Daddy was really sick. Daddy wasn't dead when they left. They wouldn't let me go to the hospital when I got home. Mama told me to come to the hospital the next day. Daddy held my hand and said, "When I get well, things are going to be really different at home. Everything is going to be just like you dreamed it would be." He made me think that he thought he might get better. That night, he was on oxygen, and he got up and went down the hall and smoked a cigarette, then went back to bed. I guess he thought, "I'll just have one more cigarette." The next morning he was dead. It was the 12th or 13th of February, 1958.

Two months before he had died, I was sitting at school on a big couch in the rec. room, and Marie was sitting there with me. We loved to talk about everything. "Marie, I am scared. I am going to tell you something. I have been praying that God would send Daddy out of town to work somewhere for the summer. I wish God would send him off somewhere to work." When he died, I felt so guilty. *Did I make him die? I prayed for him to go far away.*

I had a really bad cold and side pleurisy when I went home with Edith and Laverne. That was the only time I ever had side pleurisy. My ribs hurt so badly, and I couldn't breathe deeply. The doctor came to see me at my house. He said, "Don't go to the funeral home and the funeral, too. Just go to one, but don't go to both." I wanted to go to the funeral. When Mom went to the funeral home to look at Daddy in the casket, she fainted, and she wouldn't cry; she would just scream. Even though Mom had a hard time, she loved Daddy. She was so sick, and when she felt like she would cry, she would cough and sneeze, and her eyes would water.

On the morning of the funeral, Neva and Don came in. I had a crush on Don, and I thought he was the sweetest guy. They had a baby boy named Butchy. I thought Don was wonderful – he was the berries. When they came over, I would get real close to him on the couch. Neva didn't care, because she was talking to Mom and Daddy. Don asked me questions about school.

Don and Neva were neighbors. Neva was the daughter of Roy and May Lusby, another neighbor. Daddy and Roy were friends. One Christmas, one of Daddy's friends from Ohio, named Adrian, came to visit. He wanted to go hunting, but Daddy didn't have a license, but they went, anyway. Roy was the game warden, and he gave Daddy permission to shoot that day. Daddy shot a rabbit, but it didn't kill him. Daddy wasn't used to hunting and shooting. Roy told him to hit the rabbit with his gun. Daddy did just that, and his gun discharged in the process, shooting and killing Roy. It was a terrible tragedy, but Roy's family was so kind to Daddy and to us that we all became great friends.

When Don and Neva came that morning, I threw my hands up and started crying. "No, you will upset your mommy," Mildred, one of our cousins, said.

"She can cry all she wants. It is her daddy," Don and Neva said. Don and Neva let me cry and wiped my face. I was sick and feeling guilty.

I told Don I prayed for Daddy to die. "Margie, God has a will of His own. If He didn't want your daddy to go, He wouldn't let him go. Margie, your daddy didn't die because of your prayer."

It was so cold and snowy outside. My family asked me, "Who do you want to go to the funeral with?" "I'm going with Don and Neva," I said. Mama and I rode in the back of Don and Neva's car, and everyone was a little bothered because they weren't family. We rode to church and the cemetery. Rachel, another cousin, sang "Beyond the Sunset" for the funeral. When we started to go, Don carried me out to the car. I sat in the car at the cemetery. All the flowers were freezing. I stayed home three or four more days and then went back to school. When I got back, Judy Pierce was gone from school because her daddy had died, too.

When Daddy died, I was eighteen and in the seventh grade, and little Jody was nineteen. Mom was pinned into the house and couldn't go anywhere or do anything. She wouldn't do like some people would have and take Jody places with her. She would only take her to Aunt Dorothy's and Aunt Cleo's. Before he died, Daddy told the doctors they needed to have Mama take Jody somewhere where people could take care of her. Daddy died at age 39. He lived a life rough and hard and had cirrhosis of the liver and hardening of the arteries. His body had had so much rough treatment that he looked like an old, old man. He had heart problems that all his family had, and he had only one brother who got help with his health problems and lived until age 70. The rest of his family died at 30 or 40.

One night not long after Daddy died, Mom and Jody were at Aunt Cleo's house. It was strange to think of Jody carrying on a regular conversation, as she usually would just answer any questions asked her. On this particular night, though, she called out to Mom, "Mama, Mama." "What, Jody?" "Mama, I just hate you." "You hate me?" Mama gasped. "Why would you hate me? I've been so good to you and taken good care of you. Why do you hate me?" "Because you won't let me go to school, like Margie." Mom said it was like an answer to prayer, because she had always thought that taking her baby somewhere and leaving her would have been her undoing. Aunt Cleo was standing there and said right away, "Well, Jody, if you want to go to school like Margie, you have to learn to feed yourself." So the next morning, Jody started trying to feed herself. Mom realized she really did want to go. When they told me about it, I cried, because I knew when Jody got to Cloverbottom, which was a home for the mentally retarded in Nashville, it wouldn't be school like I went to. "It isn't fair", I said, "it just isn't fair." Back then, there were lots of little blind children who were developmentally delayed who could not go to the School for the Blind.

At Cloverbottom, there was a big room with a big circle of little rocking chairs, and all the little children sat in the chairs in the circle. They could feel that they were all there. Young people in college taking special ed were sent over there to bring in some of the outside world to these children. They would sing "John Brown's Baby Had a Cold Upon His Chest", "The Farmer in the Dell", and "Where, O Where, Has My Little Dog Gone?" Marsha Usselton was one of those students. Later, when my own little boy was about eight years old, I had the honor of working with Marsha in her own class of children at East Tennessee Rehabilitation Center in Knoxville.

There were fourteen or fifteen little blind children at Cloverbottom, and Mom got Jody into the school with the help of the doctor. Jody was so little and was still school age, so they accepted her. They had a row of little rocking chairs for the blind children. Someone would sing with them, and they would say their names. They would bring their food to them. When I was a senior, they moved Jody to Green Valley, a facility near Knoxville that was built for East Tennessee patients.

Chapter 12

I was taking voice lessons that year at school, and Mr. Donnelly had me sing, "I'm My Daddy's Sweetheart", and Miss Gray, the speech teacher, had me to play Beth in the play <u>Little Women</u>. When Mama heard me sing and saw me in the play, she cried her heart out. Mom said, "Why couldn't they give you different parts?" I wanted her to think I was good, but it made her so sad that she forgot to tell me I was good, but I loved everything I did. Miss Gray said, "If you make the people cry when Beth dies in the play, I will give you an A." Mrs. Marshall said that if I made her cry she would tell me. She was my fourth grade teacher.

Judy was Jo, and I was Beth. Margaret Ruffner played Amy, and Bonnie Merritt played Meg. My big scene included the line, "Oh, dear, dear Jo. I wish I didn't have to leave you. Take care of Marmie." I made people cry, and I got an A.

In eighth grade when we came back to school, our speech class was in a play together. I was Adele in <u>Jane Eyre</u>, and Richard was the preacher. One day the speech teacher came back stage and caught me kissing the preacher. He said, "Look, I cannot have the preacher foolin' around and kissin' on the little French girl, Adele. I'm going to have to report you to Mr. Wood."

"Oh, gosh, Mr. Donnelly, don't do that. He'll send us home," I said.

"Okay, then. I don't want any more of that going on backstage."

When Peggy was Jane Eyre, Mr. Donnelly told her to be Jane Eyre all the time, and she did. She talked so pretty, but when she came back for our alumni reunions years later, she had gone back to her country talk. I think Peggy fell in love with Mr. Donnelly.

In high school, Mrs. Wolf, our gym teacher, thought she would start out our year with a bang. "OK, girls, I want each of you blind ones to take your white cane and go on your first solo trip. I'll point you in the right direction, and you just keep on going. Now, don't use your hands for anything; just use your cane. If you come up on a bush or a tree, just touch it with your cane. Don't reach out your hand to find out what it is. I want you to learn to identify things with your cane." So off I went. Down one sidewalk, turn to the right, down another sidewalk, back to the left. *Oh, I'm getting far away from my starting point at the gym. I hadn't been that far by myself. I usually just went from the dorm to the main building. Whoops! What is this? Oh, no, I can't use my hands.* So I punched the thing in my way with my cane. I wanted to see how high it was. I traced upward with my cane and poked it a little more. "Lord, it's soft", I thought. Punch, punch. I finally found the top and bonked it. No, it wasn't the top. Boom, boom. What was it? I reached out my hand and touched a man's shirt. Yikes! "Ha, ha," I hear. "It's just me, Mr. Pitzer. I'm clearing the grass from the cracks in the sidewalk." I was so sorry. Mrs. Wolf and the girls who could see had surrounded me by then and were laughing and laughing. "Oh, little one, that was the funniest thing I have ever seen," she said. "But I told you not to use your hands."

Near the end of that year it was warm one day, and a bunch of us girls decided to go to Donelson. Mr. Wood said he didn't want us going into "Mom & Pop's" diner if any of the boys were in there. We decided to go in anyway, so we could see if any of the boys were in there. "Are any of the boys from the School for the Blind in here?" we asked. "Do you want them to be here?" the waitress asked. "Oh, we can't come in if they're here." "Well, come on in" she said. We all sat down and ordered hamburgers. We never had hamburgers at school; only good, healthy, nourishing meals, with a meat, two vegetables and a fruit, and dessert only at lunch. Oh, a wonderful, good hamburger – yum! About that time Bonnie C. looked up and said, "Oh, Lord, girls. I see E. J." That was Mr. Wood. "What!" we said. "Mr. Wood?" "Margie, I'm telling you the truth." "Do you think he's seen us? How do you know it's Mr. Wood?" "I can see his hat." Remember, the partially sighted kids couldn't see that well. A partially sighted child still only had a 20/200 corrected vision. Of course, if Bonnie could have seen Mr. Wood, he certainly could have seen us. We didn't think about that. "Oh, Lord, let's get out of here." So we all jumped up, left our hamburgers on the table, and ran toward the kitchen door. "Is there a door in here we can get out of?" "Why do you want to get out?" "Because Mr. Wood's in there, and he'll kill us if he finds us in here." That sweet black lady said, "Girls, Mr. Wood isn't in here." "Yes, he is," said Bonne, "I saw his hat." "Where?" "Right up there by the door." "Hahahahaha," she laughed. "That's a coat rack." So we all trooped back to our table and finished our hamburgers.

At recess, we would all come up to the lobby and get something from the concession stand. We'd make sure we were with our boyfriends, and then all of us would be talking to each other. The kids called me Grimley, which was the name of the frog in "Buster Brown." I heard Ronald say, "Grimley, Grimley! Come 'ere!" So I walked over to the stairs.

"What is it?" I asked.

"Move over to the right a little."

"Why? What are you doing?"

"I just wanted to give you this!" And down from the landing of the stairs came his grape drink, right on the top of my head. I was Miss Vanity as far as my hair was concerned in those days. Oh, it was sticky and purple, and I had three more hours of school to go.

Ronald was dying laughing, and he came down and said, "Shut up, Grimley! You're going to have Mr. Wood up here on me."

I said, "I don't care if I do. I will tell him he should punish you good."

"Grimley, you shouldn't do that. I was only kidding."

"When it's fun for two, it's fun, but when it's fun for only one, it isn't fun."

We had hayrides in the fall when they had a harvest moon, and we would kiss in the dark spots. Ronald would touch Richard on the back with his shoe when it was time for us to kiss. We worked hard, too, at school. Our first class was at 8:00 A.M.; band was 3:15-4:00 P.M. I would practice piano from 4:00-5:00 P.M. After supper we would have bowling or chorus. We didn't get back to the dorm to stay until 7:00 P.M. I would get into a tub of hot water for thirty minutes. I was just so tired. Then it was time to do homework. We worked hard, but we played hard, too, I guess.

I always enjoyed the trips we made from school. For one trip, our class boarded the bus to go to a museum in downtown Nashville. They wanted to show us some sculptures that a blind man had created, in case some of us wanted to pursue this as our career. We went in, and everything was very high. Ralph and Ron were telling me about everything. "Oh, Grimley, you should see this." "Oh, look at this over here." I was seeing everything through their eyes, loving it, and didn't feel I was missing a thing. Then, we came to the sculptures. Ralph said, "Grimley, I'm picking you up. You've got to see this for yourself." "How can you pick me up?" I asked. He bent down and said, "Just put your hand on my neck." He picked me up, up I went, and I was sitting on his shoulders. All the class was gathering around us, clapping. "Reach up, Grimley, and feel the sculpture." When I reached up, I touched some giant boobs! I was so embarrassed. Ron said, "That's OK, Grimley. It's educational." Then a reporter from the newspaper who was following our class for a story said, "Put your hand back up there." Ralph said, "You can move your hand down a bit, Grimley", so I did. They took our picture. When it was published, the heading under the photo read, "Classmate with sight shows blind classmate sculpture." It was a fun trip.

A few weeks later we went to Lookout Mountain in Chattanooga. We went to see Ruby Falls. Linda and Maxine were showing me the figures of fairytale characters. Marie said she didn't think she was a good describer, but I told her I thought she was. About that time, Ralph yelled, "Come here, Grimley, come here!" All of us girls went to him. "Grimley, there are stalagmites and stalactites here! Oh, Grimley, I just can't describe this to you. You just have to see it; no words can describe it!" "Ralph," I replied, "I've never wished so badly to see like you've made me want to see this." What wonderful friends they all were, and still are.

Chapter 13

Mr. Wood called me into his office one day and asked me what I wanted to do when I grew up. I told him I wanted to be an entertainer. He said, "If you're going to be an entertainer, we need to do something about your eyes." My eyes were underdeveloped and as I grew bigger, they stayed tiny and closed. Mom had never wanted to have them removed in case some miracle happened some day, and I would be able to see. But I decided I wanted them fixed, and Mr. Wood cared about me like I was one of his own, as he worried about all the kids at school. He did some research and discovered that some eye companies made little plastic shells that could be placed over the underdeveloped eyeball. They would help fill the socket and keep the lid open. Then they would place little plastic eyeballs over them. The tiny eye underneath would make them move like they were real.

The Shriners in Nashville provided my eyes. At first, they were really, really tiny, and you could hardly tell I had them in. I went back after the first month, and they made them a bit thicker. I went back in another month, and they thickened them again.

One day I fell asleep, and I dreamed that I reached out to take Richard's hand, and it was plastic. It scared me, and I jumped back.

He said, "What's wrong?"

"It's your hand. It feels like a doll hand. Only it's bigger."

"That's okay. Your eyes are plastic."

We started to kiss, and his lips were plastic. And, oh, my gosh, I had dreams like that for months, nightmares. Finally, I stopped sleeping in the plastic eyes because they were bothering me so much in my sleep that they were causing me to have these plastic dreams. I thought that was funny. Thinking back on that makes me laugh.

When I was a junior in high school, I lost one of my eyes down the drain. Mr. Pitzer had to get it out of the elbow of the pipe. Ms. Elmore took it, and boiled it. She wanted to make sure it was germ free. I don't know how it stayed the right color.

The play we did when I was a sophomore was <u>Die Fledermaus</u>. We sang a song in the play, and the words went like this: "Oh cruel bat, oh cruel bat, your jokes are getting stale and flat!" We were going to do this play, and I had always been the lead singer in chorus. It wasn't just me who thought this; all the students knew it. I had been chosen to take voice lessons, and they wanted to encourage me, because they thought I was a really good singer. So when they said we were going to do a play, we were all excited. They read out all the people's names that had parts in the play, and they called out all the names of my good friends. When all the names had been called, my name wasn't one of them. I didn't know why they didn't call my name to be a character. You know the entire choir would get to be in it as the chorus, but I was all torn up because my name didn't get called. Miss Foreman was the chorus teacher, and I went the next morning and I asked her why I didn't get a part. She said she needed me to lead the chorus. I heard that Mrs. Crocket, who was the English teacher, didn't choose me as a character because she thought I would look silly up on stage dancing with the big boys. That just broke my heart because I didn't get to be one of the characters in the play. It was a real musical.

We started practicing on the play the end of March and were to perform it the end of May. It wasn't like now when you just sort of do at it and hope it's going to go okay. We practiced enough that we *knew* it was going to go okay. About two weeks into practice, my friend Marie and I started to walk off the stage one night, and she was talking to her boyfriend. She couldn't see well, of course, but she walked in between the lights and thought I would follow her. We had big foot lights that rose up out of the floor, and my foot stepped in one, and it closed over my foot and burned my ankle really bad. I was just stood there. I guess I was numb. Ronald said, "Grimley! Git your foot out of there; it's smoking!"

"It is? It's not hurting," I said.

"Git it out!" I was trying to pull my foot out, and it wouldn't come out.

"I can't get it out!" I shouted.

"Pull your foot out of your shoe, Grimley." And I pulled it out, and he said "Oh, Lord, it's burned. It's burned." Ronald got my shoe out of the light, and two of the guys, Richard and Jerry, carried me down to the infirmary. The nurse bandaged my foot.

On my next visit to the infirmary, they said I would have to go to the hospital because there was a red streak running from my foot. Margaret Ruffner came with me, and I asked her, "Will you stay with me so that I can come back to school?"

"Yeah," she said. But when the nurses got there, she said, "Ms. Clark, here she is," and she left me. They wanted me to spend the night, and I told them, "No." Mr. Wood told them to give me a sleeping pill, and when I woke up the next morning, my face hurt from being so mad. The nurse was not very sympathetic, and she yanked that bandage off the next morning. Oh, I screamed!

She said, "Oh, you're just a big baby."

"Well, you hurt me," I said.

She let me go back to school that morning, and I had to wear a flip-flop. I walked with one foot in the grass and one foot on the sidewalk, so I could tell where I was going. I had to put my cane in the grass. Oh, my foot hurt! I stayed in the infirmary several days. Miss Foreman came down and said, "Margie, you've got to get well. You've got to come back and be in the play. I need you to lead the chorus." I was really glad that I hadn't been given a character then, because I didn't want to ruin the play. Even though it had hurt my feelings, I wouldn't have wanted to ruin the play for everyone else. I finally got well enough to go back with my flip-flop, and I led the chorus like she wanted me to, because she was afraid that someone else would forget exactly when they were supposed to come in. The play was wonderful.

During the time my ankle was burned, the band went to Washington D.C. We took a Greyhound bus, and we stood on the steps of the capital and sang. I played an E flat alto horn, which played the same thing that a French horn would play, but it was easier to play. While we were there, my foot killed me. Oh, I couldn't sleep, it hurt so badly. I was just getting more exhausted every day, but I wouldn't have missed it for anything. On the way home, we stopped at Gatlinburg, and my foot was hurting badly. I think it had gotten infected, and I asked Mr. Wood if he would call my Mama. I wanted to go home because my foot was hurting so badly. He called Mama and asked her if she would meet me at St. Mary's Hospital. I rode in the van with the boys, and Richard wanted me to put my head on his shoulder. He said he knew that Mr. Wood wouldn't get us because he knew that I didn't feel good. So I put my head on Richard's shoulder and rode all the way home, falling asleep even. Mama came and got me, and they took me into the hospital and put on all sorts of awful medicine that burned all the way from my ankle up to my knee. They sent me home. Mama had married Raymond by then. He was so nice. He made a freezer of homemade ice cream to make me feel better. After two days at home, I wanted Mama to take me back to school.

I said, "Oh Mama, I've got to go back, or I'll fail. It's exam time. You have to take me back."

She said, "I don't want to have to make a trip down there and then come right back and get you."

"Mama, you have to. I'll fail. You just call down there and ask them." She did, and they told her, "It's exam time, and you need to get her back."

I'd missed the first day of my algebra exam. I barely had a high enough grade to get by. All through school, I made A's and B's. If I took seven subjects; I would make three B's, three A's, and a C. If I tried to bring one of my B's up to an A, I would make four A's, one B, and two C's. If tried to bring my C up, I would have four A's, and three C's. I never could get them all up to A's, so on average, I had three B's, three A's, and one C. However, my algebra was a D. I was scared that I would fail. The teacher said, "I'll tell you what I'll do: I'll give you the half of the exam that they had yesterday, which is easy, and if you pass it, I'll let that be your entire exam. And if you fail it, then you fail." So I passed it. Oh, Lord, I was never so glad. Our algebra teacher, whom we called Moe, helped the people who could see and use a pencil. He would help them, and he would peck on their paper where they were doing it wrong and try to help them. The ones that were on a type slate, he'd say, "Well, I'm sorry. I can't help you." I didn't think that was fair, and I still don't think that was fair. I got through it somehow, and now I was a junior.

Chapter 14

The September of my junior year was when Linda, Lois and I formed our trio. The jazz band, The Dixie Landers, had been one of the best groups in school. We didn't know if we loved the Dixie Landers best or the wrestlers best. They were both the berries. Boy, could they play "Dixie Land!" The year after they graduated, Mr. Wood was at a loss for a group to take with him to different organizations when he visited them to tell about the school. Linda Lunsford, Lois Simmons and I had a wonderful trio. We tried our best to sound like The McGuire Sisters, and we did a pretty good job of sounding like them. We named ourselves the Starlets. One day Mr. Wood heard us singing and asked if we would like to be his group. We would go with him, he said, to tell others about our school. He would tell me what he wanted me to talk about.

"The club we are going to tonight gave us money for the trampoline, so tell some stories about the trampoline," he would tell me. I was the spokesperson, and I really told some funny stories about the trampoline. The Lions and the Kiwanis really liked those stories. Of course, I had my turn on the trampoline. I was supposed to do the feet-drop, the knee-drop and the seat-drop. When I tried the back-drop, I never could bounce up. One day, as I did the back-drop, Judy jumped on the trampoline. Instead of landing on my back, I landed on my head and fainted. "Margie, Margie, don't faint! Come back! I was just going to help you bounce up!" I couldn't sleep on my pillow for weeks. Lord, what if it had broken my neck!

The trio sang many gospel songs, and Mr. Fry took us to churches all over Goodlettsville, Dickson, and other little towns surrounding Nashville. Every church we sang at gave us a love offering. We bought ourselves a pretty blue dress alike and a nice white sweater, a red blouse, and a black wool skirt. Boy, were we Starlets!

One day, during my senior year, I went to my piano lesson, and Mrs. Cole said, "Margie, I want to talk to you. I am very disappointed."

"Why?"

"Margie, I have found out this weekend that you are an apple-polisher and a tattletale. I never thought I would find something like that out about you."

"What do you mean?" I said. "I don't even know what an apple-polisher is."

"It's what we call kissin' butt or whatever. You go in Mr. Wood's office every other day to tell what you can tell about the blind teachers."

"What? No, I don't," I said.

"Yes. My husband sits in there and hears you telling Mr. Wood."

"No," I said. "Mr. Wood tells me what to talk about when we go to the clubs." I couldn't believe that she had said that. She had been the teacher I had talked to all through school about my boyfriends. I had confided in her about everything, which even made Mom jealous. I went down to the practice room, and I cried and cried. It just tore me up. Mr. Wood came and asked, "What are you crying about?"

"Oh, I can't tell you."

"Well, then go to the Home Ec. cottage and tell Mrs. Elmore." He made me leave the building and go to the Home Ec. cottage and tell Mrs. Elmore, who was our Home Ec. teacher. I told her, and she told Mr. Wood. I told them I was going home. If I had made that big of a failure as the person that I was trying to be while I was in school, then I was going home. Even if I had passed my grades, I had still failed in everything. So I was going home. I wasn't staying, and I was calling Mom to come and get me. I called home and said, "Mama, you have got to come get me. I'm a failure. If these teachers think I'm that kind of person, you have got to bring me home. I don't care if I ever graduate. You have got to bring me home."

She came to see if I was okay and everything. I told her what Mrs. Cole had done to me. She said that she started to go in there to Mrs. Cole, but she thought if she did, then she would really bawl her out, so she tried to comfort me and make me feel okay until it was time to come home. Mr. Wood said, "I can promise you that all of your teachers don't feel like that because I know something that you don't happen to know." He knew that I had been selected by a vote from all the teachers for the Homes Award that year, an honor for the student with the most handicaps who had made the most improvement.

"You can't go home, Margie", said Mr. Wood. "Everyone would be disappointed then. You can't quit now; you're too close to the end of this long journey through school. It's been hard, and you've done well. Besides, you have to be in the play. You have to finish your voice lessons. You have to help with all the things you're planning for the Home Ec. cottage. You can't let all these people down. You're part of a team. Besides, you're going on your senior trip soon. You can't miss that."

I asked Mr. Wood if I could take piano from Mrs. Foreman for the rest of the year. "I think it would be best if you continue to take lessons from Mrs. Cole," he said. "You're about to make an upset bigger than it is." "It seems pretty big to me already", I said. "Well, it is", he said, "but we don't want to give her any more to talk about than she already has." I suppose we got more work done in piano in that two months than we had all through school, because there wasn't the usual chitchat between us. So that was a good thing.

And so, with many talks from Mr. Wood and Ms. Elmore I decided to finish out the year, and soon it was time for graduation. Dixie, my cousin from Chattanooga, Mama and Raymond, her husband, came for graduation. I wanted to go home with Dixie to see Richard, who had graduated two years before. I had gone to see him in March. Mama said, "I'm sick, and you're not going home with me? You're going to Chattanooga?"

"I'll just be there a week," I told her.

I loved Dixie. She was on my Daddy's side. She would come and get me for a week. She worked, and when she got a thirty minute break from work, she would come home and say, "Get ready! We are going to the movie." Her four kids were Linda, Billy Joe, Ricky, and Charley Man, the baby. We would watch a double feature and have snacks, then she would take us home. I never got to go to the movies at home. Movies were a part of life at Dixie's. She would also take us to the park and let us ride the rides. She would take us out to eat. Mama thought going out to eat was a waste of money.

I wore a size 3 petite when I graduated, weighed 72 pounds and was 4 feet, 2 inches tall. I went to Talladega, Alabama, a training center for the blind. Rehab wasn't going to send me to college because they said I was a "poor risk" because of my osteogenesis imperfecta. They said I'd get halfway through the year at college and break a leg, then it would all be for naught.

Chapter 15

In September, it was set up for me to go to Talladega, Alabama, for PBX training at the Adult Training Center for the Blind, where they taught independent living. You had to take your main courses from 8 a.m. until noon. Then after lunch you took classes to help you improve in your daily living, like travel and Home Ec. One thing I had to take that I hated was chair caning. You had to pull a piece of bamboo to weave a chair. It was supposed to help with switchboard, to help me follow the cords more quickly. That was the one thing I didn't like, but I really loved my switchboard trainer. She was also blind and had three children. Her name was Gerry Johnson. After the first few weeks that we were there and living in the dorm, they wanted us to move out and live on our own to see if we could do it. At that time at the School for the Blind, we didn't have the solo daily training. We had our housemothers to help with everything. Now they do teach independent living at TSB.

In Talladega, we all lived together in a dorm. The boys were on one wing and the girls were on another. We had a big common room where we could all get together. We'd sing, drink Coke, laugh and socialize in general. I am a gospel singer, so when we would get together to sing, I would always sing gospel music. Ronnie Fitts, a guy from Nashville, said, "What's wrong with you? Why don't you learn 'Satin Sheets'?" I told him, "I can sing 'I Just Do' and 'It Only Hurts for a Little While'." He said, "You're still not country!"

It was really different from high school, as we were all adults now, and no one cared if we held hands! Some of them were pairing up right off. I still thought I belonged to Richard, but it made me feel good when guys paid attention to me. Some of the guys who came were in their 30s or 40s, and some of us had just graduated from high school and were there for our post-graduate training. There was one guy named Billy Stockton, who was probably only 5 feet tall. When he met me, he immediately told me he thought I was the woman he had prayed for God to send him. I responded, "I don't think so; I already have a guy." Billy was taking piano tuning at the Center, while I was training for PBX. The piano tuning teacher came to me and said, "Margie, please pay attention to Billy, and just give him a chance. He is really smitten with you." So I said, "OK, I'll be nice to him." Then, one of the housemothers asked me if I would take a walk to get a hamburger with a new student named Junior. She told me he hadn't eaten a thing for three days. She said he watched me all the time. I laughed and said, "Sure, I'll go with him." I thought it was really wonderful that these people treated me normally, like my friends at school had. They didn't mind that I was only 4 foot 2 inches tall. "Alright, "I thought. "I am going to make it in this world." So now I had two guys to worry about. They would take us places on the bus, like music events and plays. Each of us was given a check as an "allowance". We would have the best time walking as a group to the hamburger place. All of us were taking travel training, so the staff was all for us going. They just said, "Don't hold hands, and use your own canes for the practice." Junior and Billy would both go, but there were many others who went, too, so that was OK.

Billy loved that I sang gospel music and asked me to do a duet with him at church. That was right up my alley. So, a few Sundays later we went to church together, and they asked us to do a duet. We sang, "Open My Eyes". He was so excited when we finished that he walked right off the stage and left me standing there! For some reason, that really made me mad. Of course, the preacher just said, "Come on, Margie, I'll help you down." I guess I just liked my guys to be really attentive, because I pouted for two or three weeks about that. Billy told me how much he missed me and asked if we couldn't start courting. He said he'd never do that again. I told him he was still forgetting about Richard. He said he wished I would! He wanted to kiss me, but I couldn't let him. We went home for Christmas and upon returning, he had his parents drive all over Talladega looking for me, so that he could introduce them to the girl he was going to marry! He brought me a big teddy bear. I thought, "I need to break this off right now." He begged me to let him have one kiss, and I did, but I sat there like an icebox. He said, "That wasn't like I thought it would be at all."

From two to four in the afternoon, we would take Home Ec. I flipped through my first six weeks in two weeks, but the next few weeks I didn't know anything because it was all about cooking. Mama had never even let me feel a chicken that was uncooked. I touched it, and I jumped back. Mama would let me put a piece of toast in, but she was afraid I would get burned. I could vacuum, clean windows, wash clothes, make beds, iron, separate the colors, wash dishes, and I could decorate because Mama told me about what colors go together. Here at the center, they taught us to cook breakfast. You would cook the bacon while you got in the shower, and when you got back you would cook the eggs. You weren't supposed to waste any time. I learned to fry chicken, bake a cake, cornbread, biscuits -- everything you need to know to cook.

This took six to eight weeks; then I was ready to move out of the dorm. They gave us an allowance to teach us to manage our money. We had to get our own ride to the center. I was still working on my switchboard. Mrs. Johnson, my PBX instructor, had a vacancy in her house, and she had a big flight of stairs with a room at the top that several boys rented. She had one room on the downstairs where two girls could live, across from the dining room. Then they had a private space for their family. So I moved over to her house. She had the sweetest kids. Ricky was one year old, and he was the baby. I used to rock him. Betty Jean was six. At the time, I was wearing a built up shoe, and she put on my shoes and said, "Margie, are you sure you're comfor-tull in these shoes?" I explained to her that one of my legs was shorter than the other. Ronnie was the nine year old. Mary Ruth, my roommate, and I got to eat dinner with the family, and we would wash the dishes and dry them. I stayed for six months. After three months, Mrs. Johnson said, "Margie, I just don't know if you can do this switchboard. I thought you would be faster than this." I was being really careful and was too slow. I went back to Mrs. Johnson's house and was real quiet. I started packing. She asked why I was packing. I said that I was going home because she said that I couldn't learn it. She said that she told me that to make me try harder, not to make me leave. I thought she knew more than I did, so if she said I couldn't do it, I thought that I couldn't. She said, "Well, you can do it! I didn't say it to make you leave."

Chapter 16

Midways in my stay at Talladega, Mom and Raymond came to see me. They had taken a foster child to keep. She was two years old and her name was Pam. They told her to tell me where it was that they were going. "Tell Margie where you said Daddy and Mama were taking you."

"Ala-nooga," she said. It was a mix between Chattanooga and Alabama. She was really quiet, a doll baby, and she let me hold her. When I went home, they told me that every night Pam had nightmares, but they weren't supposed to let her sleep with them, so Pam asked me if she could sleep with me! I let her think that she had to beg me. She slept with me for the first six months after I got home, and she stopped having nightmares. The people who were keeping her before had been going off and leaving her, and she felt lonely.

Human Services wanted Mama and Raymond to let Pam's mother come up and visit them, and Mama allowed it. Sarah came up and visited with us. Human Services thought that if Pam thought that Sarah was our friend, then she would like her. Then her mother ended up taking her back.

When I came home from Talladega, I met Mr. Dimpster, who was a former mayor of Knoxville. I guess he was a millionaire; anyway, he had lots of money. He was president of Employment for the Handicapped and thought it would be a good idea to take Louise Torbit, who was another blind girl, and me to some of the clubs he would be speaking at. Louise would play the piano and I would sing. It was really fun. Once when Mr. Dimpster took us to entertain, he stopped by an exclusive store in Chattanooga. He told Miss Stella Ball, his secretary, that he was going to buy Louise and me a new dress. I thought I had on a pretty dress, so I guess he just wanted to buy us something. They fitted Louise first, which was not a hard job. Then they started trying to look for the smallest dress they had in women's. I wore a size 12 in children's sizes. Miss Stella found this beautiful pink dress with embroidery all over the material. I thought it was the prettiest thing I had ever felt of, but I knew it wouldn't fit me. Mr. Dimpster said to the sales lady, "Make this fit."

"How long do I have?" she asked.

"Two hours. We'll go have lunch."

"I'm afraid I can't do that," she said.

He said, "I think you can," and he handed her a one hundred dollar bill.

"Yes, sir," she answered and started pinning those darts so that the dress would fit me like a glove. I bet that dress made me the prettiest I ever looked when I sang.

Mr. Dimpster thought I should go to college and said that he would pay for it. I was scared. I thought I might fail even though I had made A's and B's in school. I had to work hard for them. I was honest and told him I was afraid.

"But do you want to go?" he asked.

"Sure I want to go, but what if I fail?" He said he would love me just as much if I failed, but he knew I wouldn't.

I thought to myself, *Boy, I'll work hard*. Miss Ball told me not to take more than fourteen hours, but I hardly knew what she was talking about at the time. When we started figuring up my classes, I knew what she was talking about, and I only took fourteen hours.

The next year I started at Carson Newman. Richard was going for his masters at UT, and I was in my freshman year at Carson Newman. I really started to think that we would get married because we were still going together, and we were out of school. He started calling me on the phone from UT. He came up for a surprise visit. That was okay for a little bit, but I liked to rest on Saturday. I wasn't always glad to see him, but I really had to act like I was tickled. I should have known I wasn't really in love. I started to tell him, "Don't come but every other week."

"You don't want to see me?" he said.

"I am just too tired." It really upset him. He was coming to see me because he was lonely, as his family was in Chattanooga. I was tired, I guess, because I had taken on more than I could handle. I wouldn't let him hold my hand while were in the lounge at Carson Newman because it was a church school. He wanted me to come to UT where we could hold hands. When we were at UT, a teacher said, "What do you mean having her here in the lounge hugging and kissing? Do you go to college here?"

"No," I said.

"Where do you go to college? Why aren't you up there?"

"Because they don't like huggin' and kissin' up there."

"Well, we don't here, either!"

Richard said, "Don't say anything about her. She is like the Virgin Mary. She is pure. She goes to Carson Newman."

"Well, she won't be for long if she hangs around you!" replied the teacher.

We went and sat on some steps. I was feeling embarrassed, because the teacher corrected us for hugging and kissing.

Then summertime came. One day we were at UT, and we decided to catch the bus and go to Chattanooga. I had to wait until we were there before I called Mom to tell her.

"I will be back on Monday," I told her, and she had a fit that I didn't tell her we were going. I came back Monday to Carson Newman, and they picked me up.

Richard and I dated for eight years, and we loved each other, but he ended the relationship because he said, "I have to marry a girl who can see. I would be too scared for me and you to cross the street together." Richard called me on the phone years later, after I was married, telling me that he was ill. He wanted me to come see him, but I refused. I asked him if he was saved, and he said that he didn't want to talk philosophy. I ended the conversation, and he died six months later.

I loved Carson Newman, and I made better grades than in high school. It took me a long time to read my lessons in high school. I would have to read them all twice in order to make a good grade, A's and B's. I had all A's in college. I would put on the board, "If anyone is interested in reading their English out loud for pay, see me after class." During the second semester, a senior would come and read on my recorder. It was really good to have that for my English. I wasn't able to take gym in college because it was really wearing me out. I wasn't strong enough.

I was majoring in church music with my emphasis on voice. My minor was social work. They didn't have much about special ed. or else I would have taken that. We took the Cotter Preference Test, and it said that I was really interested in social work. At school you had to take one language besides Italian, which you had to learn for songs in your voice classes. I started out taking French, but it was hard because the things didn't sound like you spelled them. Before it got too late in the semester I started taking German instead of French. I did a lot better in German. Our professor loved Germany, and she would tell us about the beautiful scenes there. I got a reader who was from Germany. She had married Professor Covey who was a German teacher. She knew exactly how to pronounce everything in German. That Christmas, the whole German department was going to stand out under a tree decorated for Christmas and sing "O Tanenbaum" and other Christmas songs in German. I was so excited that we were going to sing, and I ran to my room to get ready and accidentally put lotion in my hair and hair spray on my hands! It wasn't because I was blind; it was just because I was excited. I just yanked up the bottles and squirted and scrunched. Then I said, "Oh no, what will I do now?"

One day it was raining, and I was walking across campus with my book satchel, which was too heavy for me to carry in one arm, along with an umbrella and my white cane in the other hand. When you have an umbrella over your head, it blocks out your optical perception or facial vision. There was a truck sitting in front of the steps to the administration building. I was going towards it as fast as I could go. I was just about to run into it when four students came and grabbed me at the same time. All of them were coming from different directions, and none of them knew that the other was watching me. They all started running and reached me at the same time. When they grabbed me, it scared me to death! "What's wrong?" I hollered. We all stood there in the rain laughing when they told me I was just about to run over a truck. I would have had black eyes for a month! That night I thanked God for letting them care about me, and I felt safe on campus from that moment on. I knew the campus pretty well, but I usually walked with the girls to the dining hall. If we wanted something to eat in the student center when they opened it at 8:30 p.m., all us girls would put our raincoats over our pajamas and go get something to eat because we didn't want to have to put back on our clothes. I will always think about Carson Newman when I hear the song "Summer Place" or drink a cherry coke.

Chapter 17

I loved Carson Newman so much that I decided to go during the next summer so that my load wouldn't be so heavy in the fall. I took two semesters of English that summer. I met and made lots of good friends.

I had my dummy by this time. Mr. Ben Lockhart, a man that lived in Mom's neighborhood, said that he would share his ventriloquist's secrets with me, and I might be able to make some money. He had seen me when I went to the school and did an impersonation of a mother and a baby for some kids. He said that if I could do that, then I could do ventriloquism. He said that he would sell me a dummy. Their faces were made of plaster of Paris and would crack easily. The one that he sold me was one that had been remade. He was a neat dummy. I did loads of programs and Bible stories with him. His name was Rick.

There were lots of small churches around Jefferson City and counties close by. The college would send out the students who were taking courses in religion and Bible to pastor the little churches. They would invite me to come sing and give my testimony and tell a Bible story with my dummy. Some of the people at Carson Newman would invite me home on the weekend to their home churches to sing. I loved it!

My legs were very fragile, and I had to walk even more at college than at the School for the Blind. I started having lots of pain in my legs. In January, I started the second half of my sophomore classes. I ended up taking lots of BC headache powder and anything else that would help the pain. I would take a BC before I would walk to the next class. Finally, I ended up in the infirmary, and I missed a whole day, which meant cuts in every class. I told my teachers what happened, and they didn't count the cuts. During spring break, I went home and went to the orthopedic doctor, Dr. Bob Patterson, who sent me to the Crippled Adult Hospital in Memphis. He wanted to know why I went a year and half before I came to him. I said that I was afraid that he might not let me go to college. He said I was right. If I went back I had to go in a wheelchair. At the hospital, they were deciding whether they were going to do surgery on my legs. They were crooked at the top and crooked at the bottom, and they were going to straighten them. They said it would make me four to five inches taller, but I couldn't decide. It would mean a stay in the hospital of a year, and I was afraid that somebody would steal Richard. There were 49 doctors at the hospital, and all of them had to vote affirmatively about the surgery in order to do it. They had me climb up a ladder and look at my legs and everything. I was having trouble with my knee joints and my hip joints. When the leg is crooked, it makes the joint pull apart on one side, and all the weight was on one side of the joint as I walked. They said that was why my knees hurt. I wanted to go back to Carson Newman, and I decided that I wouldn't go back in a wheelchair. There was a girl in wheelchair at that time in college, and I would hear the girls talk about pushing her. Her name was Wanda, and one day I heard a girl say unhappily, "Oh, it's my day to push Wanda."

I said, "I thought y'all liked Wanda."

"We do, but we hate it when it's our day to push her."

"Why?" I asked.

"Because we have to go in a different door when we push her." Carson Newman wasn't made that handicapped accessible. I thought, *Oh, I am never going to come up here in a wheelchair if they feel like that.*

"Why don't you bring her across the dining hall when you bring her, and then you can talk to everybody. She would like it, too." They did that a time or two, and then they stopped. I don't know if somebody in the dining room said that they couldn't or what, but that convinced me that I would never go there in a wheelchair, because I didn't want the girls to feel like they had to push me if they didn't want to. But Wanda did, and she went, and she got her education, and she didn't care if they didn't want to push her. She just acted like they did.

The doctor told me that I could go back if I went in a wheelchair, but I didn't want to. I wanted to be able to walk and be independent, so I said I wouldn't go back. Some people understood that if my legs were that exhausted, then the rest of me would be, too. I wanted to finish college in four years, and if I couldn't, I said that I just wouldn't go back. I was so stubborn. I went back to get all my books and everything, and it just broke my heart that I wasn't going back, but still I was too stubborn to go in a wheelchair. I went and told all my teachers goodbye, and I went home. I was tired when I went home, and I went to bed and slept 'til the next morning. When I woke up, I ate breakfast and went back to sleep. I slept day and night for a week.

So, I didn't get to go back to Carson Newman, and they didn't do the surgery because I went home for them to think about it, and for me to think about it. I wrote a letter to them and said that, as far as I was concerned, if they felt that they should do the surgery, I would be willing because God had made my legs strong enough to walk once before. If He could do it once, then He could do it again. When they replied, they said that if God could make my legs walk, then they weren't messing with them. I thought I was giving them permission, but I guess I wasn't. Mama said, "I knew they wouldn't when I read that letter."

I wish that I had had a wise counselor who would have told me that I could go back in September. Now, I think that if I had gone back and majored in Special Ed., I could have taught little children, preschool blind children. In different towns they have classes set up for preschool blind children, and the parents have a choice whether to send them to the School for the Blind or the preschool in their town or a public school. Later on, I did get to work in the preschool at East Tennessee Children's Rehabilitation for Preschool Blind Children. I loved it. I loved working with Debbie and Marsha in Knoxville, and I am thankful I had that experience.

Chapter 18

I came home to Mom, Raymond and the little girl they had through foster care named Pam. Raymond had been a bachelor, and he didn't have any kids. He loved kids, so Mom and he decided that they should adopt a child because Mom had had surgery so that she couldn't have any more babies because Jody and I were handicapped. I was grown up, and I thought, *Well, if he and she want to adopt a kid, well, okay.* Then one day Mama said, "Well, I think I have a right to have some healthy kids, don't you?" That hurt my feelings. She didn't mean for it to hurt my feelings; she just wanted me to agree with her. It hurt my feelings because I wasn't her healthy kid, and she felt like she needed to still have a healthy kid to learn how it really was.

Later, Mom and Raymond went to the Human Services office and applied to adopt another little girl. They talked to them about different children. They told them about Judy, a four year old, and Mom and Raymond went to Greenville to see her. At first Human Services thought that she wouldn't be adoptable because she couldn't say any of her words, but now she could say some of her words, and so they adopted her. She was a little chubby girl, real cute. They had her on a diet making her drink buttermilk and other things she didn't like. She had been in an orphanage and thirteen foster homes. No one would keep her, but Mama didn't know all that. They gave her Judy's history, and Mom and Raymond agreed to keep her for a year, and then sign to adopt. Mama said that her home wasn't going to be the fourteenth for Judy, and she planned to keep her from the start.

Pam and Judy were the same age. I had already fallen in love with Pam when she was about two, when I would come home from Carson Newman in the summer. They were both four years old now, and I loved them to death. Since I was out of college by then, I gave them all my time. Judy couldn't say anything plainly, and you had to work to understand everything she said. I would hold her on my lap and help her learn to say things. They had told that little girl before we adopted her, "If you don't learn to talk plain, nobody will adopt you." So, boy, she worked on that speech.

I would say, "L-ook."

She would say, "W-ook."

"Don't move your lips. Move your tongue. Now watch my mouth. Put your tongue at the roof of your mouth, L-L-L-L."

"W-W-W-W." But finally she learned to say "look", and we continued to work on "L" words. "Put the 'l-ook' sound onto it. L-ook."

"L-ook, l-ove," she would say. I would hold her on my lap for hours and work with her. When it was time for her to go to school, Mama told them she might need a speech class, and they said,

"Why?" I had already taught her how to say everything. I was glad that I had gotten to give her that gift. Her life would have been a lot worse if I hadn't. She loved me, too, and she still loves me, but she faced many obstacles as she became an adult.

Now about Pammy. Raymond worked at the Standard Knitting Mill, and he would go by the house where she lived with her real mother sometimes just to see if he could see her. He just wanted to know if she was okay. Human Services had taken her back to her mother, and we were worried about her because we knew in our hearts that she was ours. One day Raymond went by there and saw her looking out the window, and Lord, she saw his car and she came running out yelling, "Daddy, Daddy!" He stopped because he saw her running toward the street. He got out, and he picked her up and loved her. She cried and cried, "Don't leave me! Don't leave me."

Her mother Sarah was there and said, "Well, do you want to take her home with you?" He said, "Yeah, if it's okay with you." So Daddy put her in the car and brought her home. When they got there, he said, "Hey, Elma, come here and look who I've got." We ran in there, and it was Pammy. We were so tickled. After that, Judy would beg us to go get the little girl to play with her. We started going to get her on some weekends. Sarah said that Pam begged for us all the time, and they had to take her around on the bus to keep her calm.

When they were six, and it was time for them to go to school, Sarah Lou called Mama and asked, "Would you keep her and send her to school?"

"We love her, and you know we love her. I will keep her and send her to school, but if you try to come get her and take her away from us, I will fight every court in the land to keep you from getting her. If I start her to school, I'm finishing this year of school. Don't you dare come and get her until next summer, if you come and get her."

"I won't be back, Mrs. Elma." Sarah Lou had saved money, and she brought a dozen little dresses she had bought for Pammy. She hung them on a rack behind the stove to keep them safe, and they were all dirty, so Mama had to wash them. Sarah wasn't thinking that they would get dirty. She just hung them there so that they would be safe.

Pam and Judy would go down to the road and catch the school bus. We thought they were getting along good, but every year older they got, the more scrambles they got into. Their first year of school Pam's teacher was Mrs. Cates. She was the sweetest thing, and we all loved her. They said "Don't put Pam and Judy in the same class," so Judy was in Ms. Goodman's class, and she was a little harder on the kids than Mrs. Cates was. Pam was drawing pictures, and her teacher called Mama one day and said, "Mrs. Hickman, I want you to come down here. Pam's pictures are worrying me." We were all torn up. *Something was wrong with Pammy, strange things. She must be emotionally disturbed.*

Mama got down there, and Pam was drawing all these pictures with horns on these people's heads. "I don't know why she would be drawing horns on people's heads," Mama said.

Then the teacher said, "She sits here and watches this woman hang up her clothes rather than watching what I'm writing on the board. She's looking out the window."

Pam said, "Them's pretty, Mama. She's got pretty clothes to hang up."

Mrs. Cates said, "She is supposed to look at the board. I can't keep her attention for nothing." I thought Judy would be the one to have trouble, but our Pammy was having trouble. Well, one day, Donna, a girl I went to college with, came over to visit me, and said, "Show me Pam's pictures." So Mama showed them to her, and she said, "Pam, who is this?"

"Margie," she answered.

"You drew Margie? What is that?" she asked, pointing to the things over my head.

"That's her arms," Pam said.

"Well, draw the arms coming out right here. Don't draw them coming out the ears." She showed her where to put the arms, and Pam never drew horns again.

So, in the end, Mom and Raymond adopted both of them. Pam was twelve before they adopted her, after her mother died.

Chapter 19

The next summer, I went to Camp Easter Seals in Old Hickory, TN. There I met a whole bunch of people who were handicapped. Some of them had polio or muscular dystrophy. One man had no arms. He would hold stuff with his feet, and he was just as jolly as anything. There was a girl there, Linda, who was sweet. Her family didn't want her because she was in a wheelchair, so she went to the Home for the Incurable in Memphis. Linda had a job as a secretary there. Debbie had had polio when she was a little girl, and she told about being in the iron lung. She was really slim. When she went for lunch she would only eat twelve bites. She said that she wouldn't eat because no one could lift her if she gained weight. Eddie Deaver and Eddie Scarborough were both from Knoxville.

At the camp we had a wheelchair prom. Tonya asked Eddie Deaver, and the other Eddie asked me to be his date. They put up crepe paper and made the dining room all pretty. I wrote home and had Mom send my formal dress. I hadn't known to bring one, but it got there in time. At the prom, Eddie asked me to dance. I didn't know how to dance with someone in a wheelchair. He said, "Just hold my hands," and we danced, and he said I was a good dancer. We had a good time.

When I came home, Mt. Harmony Church on Strawplains Pike, just a mile from Mom's house, had a new choir director, Bob Nicely. He and his wife and three sons had all come there to go to church. It was the church Mom grew up in. I was still in the college mode, so I thought that I should write down all the songs in Braille if I was going to sing in the choir. The girls in the neighborhood would come and dictate the hymns to me, and it helped me get to know the young teenage girls, which was good for them and for me.

While I was at Camp Easter Seals, the people there had told me about the Club for Handicapped Adults. It met at the Presbyterian church in Knoxville. I started going there once a month, and I met lots of handicapped people there. I met a guy named Don Mauldin. He talked very polished and was really nice. He asked me if I wanted to sit by him when we ate. He pulled out my chair and told me what was on my plate. He was partially sighted. He had gone to the School for the Blind in Alabama. After two months of going to the club, he asked me if I would go on a date with him. I said, "How would we go?" He said he would get his mother and daddy to pick me up and drop us off at a movie.

When we went to the movie, he said that he had to go to the restroom, and he wanted to know if I needed to go, too. I said, "Yes," but when he took me downstairs and left me at the restroom door, I started to worry because I didn't know his voice very well yet. I thought, *What if the wrong person comes to get me?* But, of course, the wrong person didn't come after me, and everything was just fine.

We went back upstairs and we watched the movie, <u>Doctor Zhivago</u>. Afterwards, when we were driving up to my house, he wanted to kiss me in the backseat. I didn't want to, because his mom and daddy were in the front seat. He kissed me, but just for a second. When we got my house, he walked me to the front porch and kissed me again.

Don and I started going together, but his mom didn't want him to go with me. My mom didn't know anything about his mother not wanting us to go together. Then one day, I came home and said, "Mom, Don asked me to marry him." "You can't get married. You can't do everything you need to do in a house," Mama said. Raymond said, "Elma, she's twenty-eight years old. You can't tell her that she can't get married."

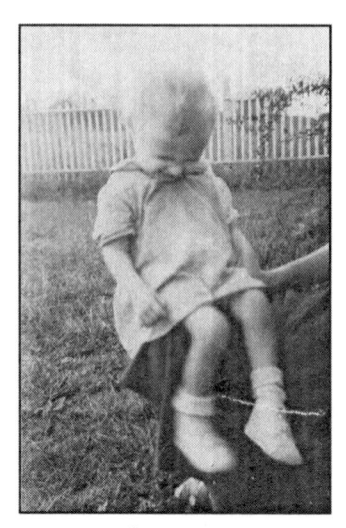

Baby Margie

Jody and parents–1954

Margie and her mother

Margie and Jody–1957

Margie in leg braces

TSB band, with Margie front and center

"The Starlets"–Lois Simmons, Margie, Linda Lunsford

Tennessee School for the Blind Class of 1962

Training in Talladega

First-time bride–1968

Margie and Rick

Margie and David

Margie and Kelly

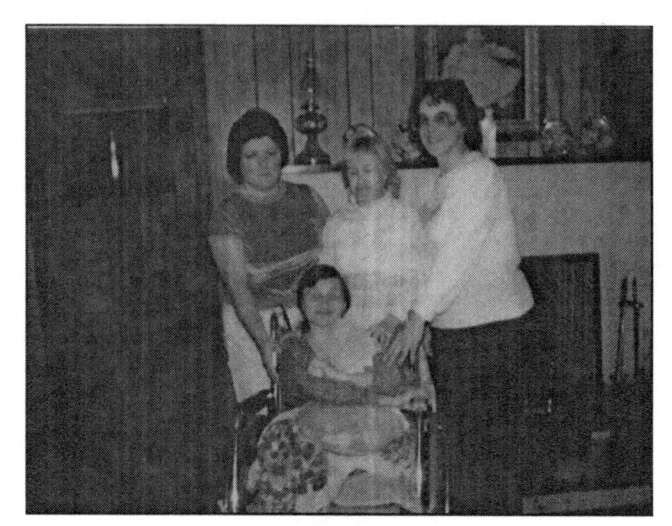

Margie and her sisters—Judy, Pam and Jody

Margie and Billy—April 6, 1998

56

David, Billy, Margie, Jody

David and Joseph

Chapter 20

After I had attended the Easter Seals camp, Mr. Davis, the manager of Easter Seals in Knoxville, said that they would pay for my voice lessons if I found someone who could teach me. Mr. Harry Hall from Broadway Baptist church said that he would be my voice coach. At this time, people were inviting me to their churches to sing, and my cousin, Vicky, would play the piano for me. I never expected a love offering, but most of the time, I was given one. Vicky and I would go shopping to buy new dresses to sing and play the piano in. On a particular day when Vicky and I were shopping, a lady named Mrs. Joann Newman stopped me and asked me why I was so happy. "Well, there's nothing to be sad about," I said.

"But you're blind," said the woman. "What makes you happy?"

"I love to sing. Someday I want to make an album for the Lord."

"My husband has a recording studio where people make records. Here is his card."

I called him, and he told me to come down and talk to him about making my album. I began saving my love offerings, so that I would have enough money to pay Mr. Newman. On the day I was supposed to go make my album, I counted my money, and I lacked fifty dollars. "Oh, God, if it's Your will for me to make this album, please let me know what to do."

I went to Mom and asked if she had paid the light bill yet. "Why do you need to know that?" she said. Most moms would have been jumping up and down, because they would have been excited about me making an album. "Mama, please let me borrow fifty dollars until I go to the next church and get another love offering."

"What do you mean?" she said. "Four people besides you live in this house."

"Mom, you know I'll give it back."

"Oh, no, you won't , because you aren't getting it." It broke my heart, because I felt that Mama had no faith in me. The two little girls, Judy and Pammy, came in and loved me because I was sad, and the three of us went out to the mailbox when the mail came. As we got the letters out of the mailbox, Pammy said, "This letter says 'Margie'. "

"How do you know it says 'Margie'?" I asked.

"I see the big 'M'."

"Oh! Oh, alright!" We got in the house, and I opened the letter. "Daddy," I asked, "is this a check?"

"Yep, that's what it is," he said.

"How much, how much?"

"Fif-ty," he said. It was a love offering check from a church I had sung at recently. So I put the fifty dollars with the rest of my money and went to the Newman Studio. Mr. Hall, his wife and I all went to the Newman Records Studio where I made my first album. Don and I had just gotten engaged, and he wanted to go with me. I could tell that, for some reason, Mr. Hall didn't seem to like Don much. He said if I had to bring him with me, then I had to tell him to be quiet. I just thought Mr. Hall was being hateful.

Mrs. Hall played the piano. It was rinky-dink, and she wasn't too happy with it, but we did get that record made. I titled it I'll Walk with God. When the record came back all finished, I went from house to house on Osborne Road, Eds Road, Pine Grove Road, Strawplains Pike. Little Pam and Judy were so excited, and they walked all the way with me. I sold a bunch of those albums. I also took a box to Mt. Harmony Baptist Church to sell. They cost $5.00. Then, every time I went somewhere to sing, I took records to sell. By the time Don and I went to Newport to Hoyte Staton's furniture store, I had the money to buy all the furniture for our pretty apartment.

Soon after that, people began to invite me to their churches to sing. I was thrilled because, finally, I was going to do something for God, which is what I had wanted to do most of all with my life. I wanted to walk the walk and talk the talk.

When Don told his parents that we were getting married, they told him no. He got mad and threw the popcorn popper across the room. They said, "Okay then, marry her!" They took us out to look at apartments, saying that I probably wouldn't marry him when it came time anyway. They took us to Newport to my cousin's furniture store where we bought end tables, a coffee table, and an off white couch and chair, all in French Provincial, because Don's stereo was French Provincial.

The apartment we rented in Knoxville was at the Shenandoah Apartments on Casswell Pike, near the Greenwood Cemetery and Smithwood Church. The grocery store was close enough to walk to, but we had to be careful, as it was a very busy road. Mr. Bailey, our landlord, invited us to attend services with him at the Smithwood Church.

The great room in our apartment had a very peaceful atmosphere. It was a long room, so we fixed a living room in one end and a dining room in the other. We bought a table and six chairs, a hutch with open shelves at the top and drawers and doors at the bottom. We bought a leather couch and chair for the room we used as a den. The couch made a bed because I knew the girls, Judy and Pam, would be coming for visits. We got a pole lamp, a nice TV stand, and I can't remember what else. I had a new bedroom suite in my room at home, which we were going to bring, along with my piano. Don's mother said she had never seen anyone go buy the whole house full of furniture at once.

We started bringing our clothes and hanging them in the closet, mine in the bedroom, and Don's in the den. Mom didn't want me to bring them until we were married, but Don's parents were bringing his, so I wanted to bring some of mine, too. I loved being with the girls and reading stories to them, singing songs with them, and Raymond would take me to voice lesson every Monday. Home was happy, but I wanted so bad to get married like everyone else that I didn't want to wait. Don and I got married on Friday, May 10, 1968. I was 28 years old. I weighed 79 lbs. and was 4'2". That morning, Mom dropped me off at the beauty parlor to get my hair done. They fixed my hair really pretty and polished my nails. They said, "Now go home and put a silk pillowcase on your pillow and rest until the girls get home from school." So I did just what they said – laid down on a silk pillowcase and went promptly to sleep. Mom was at church. The wedding cake had been delivered there, and some mice had been seen earlier, so she wanted to protect it. Mammaw Hughes had provided the wedding cake. The girls would be home around 3:00 with Mom, who always went and picked them up. The next thing I knew Mom ran into my room screaming, "Margie, how could you do this? How could you? I was there watching your cake, and you didn't even call me to pick up the little girls from school, and you laying here asleep." "Mom, I didn't know you'd forget to get the girls!" "Well, you could have been doing something besides laying here sleeping." *Oh, well,* I thought, *there's my wedding day excitement.* Every time I would get excited about something, Mom would say, "Don't get too excited; it hasn't happened yet," and boom -- there would go my excitement. Still to this day, I get excited before something happens.

We had a beautiful wedding at Mt. Harmony Baptist Church. We used daisies, the church was decorated pretty, and I had a big wedding cake. Mr. Hall sang "Entreat Me Not to Leave Thee." Then we were whisked away to our fully furnished apartment.

Chapter 21

After the wedding, we went straight to our apartment, because I wanted to know my way around. Camp Easter Seals said that we could have the honeymoon cottage if we wanted. I turned it down, because I didn't know how we would have gotten groceries and other things that we needed, and I didn't know my way around there. That was silly; they probably would have taken care of us. They wanted me to be the Easter Seals girl, but I wanted to be my own girl. They wanted me to call my album You'll Never Walk Alone and put me on their poster, but I wanted it to be I'll Walk with God, which said the same thing, but I was young and stubborn.

For the first eight months of our marriage, Don and I never had a short word with each other. I was still doing my programs with the dummy, going to every church that invited me to sing and tell Bible stories. I was really, really happy. I thought Don's temper had completely disappeared. *Why, he loves me so much, he's changed*, I thought.

At the apartment complex, they were supposed to clean out a storage place downstairs for your big stuff that you didn't have room for, but they still hadn't done that. We had a beautiful first Christmas, and about two or three days after Christmas, I took the flu. I was so sick that I could hardly sit up, and I had a fever of 103. I had been helping Don with his snack shop on Sunday afternoons, and that week, when I said I couldn't go, that he needed to call his mommy and daddy to come help, he got really angry with me and said that I had to go. And so I went. As soon as I agreed to go, his anger was gone.

About the middle of January, when I felt like doing things again, I took our Christmas tree down, and put up the decorations, and put the tree in the box. I pushed the box in the bedroom and vacuumed the living room. I was really proud of myself for getting things done again. I picked up all the shoes out of the floor of my closet and shoved the Christmas tree box in the closet and made a shelf of it. I was pleased and thought it could just stay right there all the time. I was tired when I got all that done but pleased, too. When Don came in from work, I said, "Look what all I got done today!" I showed him what all I got done, and he saw the Christmas tree box in my closet.

He said, "Why did you do that?"

"I put it all up," I said.

"Why did you put it in the closet? You know they're supposed to make a place to store it in the basement."

"I don't mind it," I said. He grabbed his keys and ran to the door. He was going to tell Mr. Whitt a thing or two. I started crying, and I grabbed his keys. He grabbed me and shook me. There went the end of that dream of peace. I sat in the chair and cried with a headache. Now I knew that his temper hadn't really gone away. But things got good again, and it was a while before he had another temper fit.

It's been a long time since all that, so I can't remember what all his temper tantrums were about, but I still thought our home was good enough to raise a child. So I started praying that God would help me find a baby. I went to the birth defect clinic on the advice of my gynecologist. He said, "Go to the birth defect clinic, and they will tell you how much of a chance your baby will have of inheriting the osteogenesis imperfecta." I was afraid they would tell me not to have my own baby, and I wanted that more than anything in the world. I went to Dr. Jerdan at Four-way Inn who was my primary physician when I lived at Mom's house. He said if I became pregnant, he would do a C-section and take my baby when it weighed five pounds, so that we wouldn't have to worry about breaking my pelvis in giving birth. That sounded good to me.

When I went to the birth defect clinic, they did all kinds of tests such as physicals. They put a bag over my head and took pictures of me in the nude, so that doctors could look at my body to see how crooked my legs were, and that my neck is short, and my waistline is short. They were really getting personal, but I was willing to go through it if it meant finding out if my baby would be blind and have brittle bones. Don and I had a big fuss, because his mother wanted him to have a vasectomy. I said he had to wait until I got the results of the chromosome test back. His mother didn't want him to wait. She was afraid I would stop taking the birth control pills and get pregnant. When the birth defect clinic said they needed information about Don, too, his mother said they couldn't have it. I said, "What's the matter? Do you have something to hide that I don't know about?" So she finally gave them the information. Of course, it was kept confidential from me. When the results of the chromosome test came back, nothing was wrong. So I said, "I'm going to go ahead and have my baby." They said that something might be wrong with my genes, but they couldn't take that test yet.

I applied with Human Services to adopt a baby. At that time in Knoxville Human Services was against letting a blind couple adopt a baby, so my caseworker did lots of extra home visits to see if we were fit to adopt a child. I made lunch for her, took her to see where Don worked, and told her of all my plans about how I would take care of my little baby. I told her how Aunt Dorothy had let me diaper her babies, give them baths, dress them, and, of course, rock them to sleep. I would feed my baby with an infant feeder until he learned to sit up. The caseworker was young and thought it all sounded wonderful, but her supervisors didn't think it was so great. Don and I thought we would be interested in adopting a handicapped baby, since we would know better how to take care of a handicapped child than people who were not handicapped. Both of our parents had a fit. They said that they had had enough handicaps in their lives. So when Human Services turned us down, I was emotionally distraught. I thought I was not worth anything. *Nobody thinks I can take care of a little child. I don't care about anything anymore.* I told everyone that, and went home, and went to bed. I stayed in bed and cried for six weeks.

One night Don came in from work and said, "Get up out of that bed right now. Get dressed and comb your hair. We are going out to eat and then shopping at the K-Mart." I was scared of Don when he was mad. I thought of asking him for a divorce. I could go home and help Mom raise the girls, but instead, I made it to supper and the K-Mart. It did feel good to get out of the house. Each time I would go to church to do a program, sing, give my testimony, and tell a Bible story for the children, I would ask them to pray that God would bring me a child. I adapted my testimony to fit that desire of my heart.

I stayed in bed for about six weeks and hadn't given my testimony for that long. I was really depressed. I had been going to churches everywhere to sing, tell Bible stories and give my testimony. I told Bible stories that Mom used to tell to me when I was 3 or 4 years old – Moses, Daniel, David, and of course, the baby Jesus. The cross made me cry. When I gave my testimony I would tell how I saw colors in my mind, because people were always asking me what I thought about colors. Here's what I would say:

> I will start with black. Black is all colors wrapped into one. It is very thick, coarse, and dark. People can hide in its darkness, or they may rise above it with a beautiful personality that sparkles and shines out of it. At this point they can feel sophisticated. White is very smooth, so smooth that it's almost slick, but it's not a shiny slick because it is so pure, so free. As I am blind, I am prone to wear white slacks with many outfits because I like white better than black. My friends say, "I couldn't wear white slacks for anything. I'd get a spot on them right away," but I don't worry about that. My next color is pink. I have pink shoes and pink tops and skirts with lots of color with splashes of pink that my tops bring out. Pink is very soft and delicate. I love the light, light pink, because I want it to be soft. I used to think of soft as little baby dresses. Their little faces feel so sweet against that softness. Blue is for little boys and is a little thicker. It reaches to the sky. It's a dreamy color, not like pink that cuddles around you, but wider and more spread out. I hear blue water when I go to the lake or the ocean and I feel the blue sky when the wind gently glows, like in Savannah. You can see what I'm doing – I feel my colors, not just with my hands but with my heart. Green – I love green. It's like grass smells just after daddy finishes mowing. It smells so springy and summery. Orange is like an orange sucker tastes. Red is like a crackling fire, and you have to stand close to keep the chill away. It's a happy color for Christmas and Valentine's Day. I guess red is a party to me! I have a beautiful red blouse with little jewels across the front at the waistline. Yellow is like the sunshine. Every time I go outside and the sun is shining, it makes me smile, and I start singing, "Sunshine on my shoulders makes me happy…" Gold and silver are shiny colors. They are both happy colors, but silver is a much smoother, slicker kind of shiny. If I could see all of a sudden, I might not recognize my colors, but they satisfy me at this time. I tell about miracles and say they are still the same today, because God is the same yesterday, today and forever. But I think of myself as being like Paul, when God said to him, "My grace is sufficient for you, for power is perfected in weakness." Maybe I'm a better witness as I may be stronger with being blind. When I was 12 years old I prayed for God to help my legs be strong enough to walk. He did that, and I was able to go to school and graduate, to go to Talladega for business course, and to Carson Newman College for 18 months.

This is the testimony I gave from college until the time I started wanting a baby. At that point I added a prayer request each time, that all those in that church would pray for God to send me a baby.

Chapter 22

A friend, Sherrie Williams, came to visit me. I loved her so much when we were in school. She was a doll baby and would come to visit me in the summer when school was out. When I told her my story about wanting a baby, she cried along with me. She said, "What can I do to help you, Margie?"

"Well," I answered, "your mother works in a restaurant at night, right?"

"Yes, but what does that have to do with anything?"

"Well, my cousin Dixie, who lives in Chattanooga, says that lots of times, pregnant girls come into her restaurant at night. They are crying and have no place to go and don't know what to do with their baby. So I thought your mom might have the same experience." Sherrie said she didn't think that would happen. But she would tell her mom, and if it did happen, of course, they would call me.

My prayer at this time was: "Dear God, please, if You want me to have a baby, help me to find one. And Father, if you do not want me to have a baby, please take away this strong desire. I crave a baby, Lord. I just want to give it love. And of course, I will teach it all about you, God, and how Your Son came to die for us all."

Just about that time, Don's Aunt Anne sent some sheet music to me. The title of the song was "His Way Mine." The lyrics go as follows:

God has a place for every planned creation,
A path for every star to go.
He drew the course for every river's journey.
Now I know he makes a plan for me.
I place my life in the hand of God,
Those hands so scarred, outstretched for me.
Wherever I may be, over land, over sea,
May Thy will sublime, oh dear God divine, be mine.
Now in His will, my soul finds life worth living.
Each day, new blessings from above.
Though shadows come and valleys seem unending,
Still I know He makes a way for me.

And I found myself meaning the words in that song.

About three months after Sherrie's visit, she called me on the phone. "Margie, oh Margie, I think I've found you a baby!" she said.

"Sherrie, I'm doing lots better, but don't tease me. I'm not that well yet."

"I would not do that," she said.

"Is it a boy or a girl?" I asked.

"We don't know. It isn't born yet."

"Oh, oh, she'll change her mind before it's born."

"I don't think so," said Sherrie. "Do you want this baby no matter if it is a boy or girl?"

"Yes, yes, yes!"

"Well, then my friend Shirley who is carrying your baby will be calling you soon."

I ran and told Don, and even he seemed excited. "You're going to be a daddy," I said.

One night about three in the morning, Shirley called me. I asked her, "Will you change your mind because I'm blind?"

"No. I'm staying at Sherrie's house until it's born, and I get to see how she does everything. If you are as smart as Sherrie is, then I'm not worried at all!"

"Well, I can take care of it, if that's what you're wondering about."

"I believe you," she said. "You see, half of one of my arms was gone when I was born. People said I couldn't take care of my little girl, but I was able to show them."

"You have a little girl?"

"Yes, Mama has her right now."

"What if she wants this baby?"

"She doesn't know I'm pregnant," she said. I asked her how far along she was, and she said four months. We talked to each other about every two weeks, and when she was seven months pregnant, I asked her if she had gone to the doctor, and what did he say? When she said she hadn't been to the doctor, I started to panic. I talked to Mom and told her that Shirley hadn't been to the doctor. She thought I ought to call a lawyer friend of hers. So I called him. He said he knew that I would be a good mother, but if Human Services wouldn't let us adopt though them, they might come and try to take the baby away from me. So he said the best idea was for Shirley to go into the hospital as me.

"What if she decides she wants the baby back someday?" I asked him.

"Is she rich?" he asked.

"No," I said.

"Well, then that's still your best bet."

I wanted this baby more than anything in all the world. I prayed and prayed about it. There was complete peace in my heart, and when David was born he was mine. Shirley, the woman who gave birth to him, thought he would be born about the middle of April, and when he wasn't born yet, I was afraid she had decided to keep him. But on the 16th of May, I received a phone call telling me that I had a healthy baby boy. I was so excited. There are no words to express it!

When David was three days old, Brenda and her husband Mickey said they would take me to Nashville to pick up my baby. At Sherrie's house, Shirley laid David on the bed, and Sherrie's mother Hazel picked him up and brought him to place him in my arms. I almost went into shock. *Thank you, God*, I said in my heart. That baby lay so still and quiet, as if he knew that something important was taking place. I brought a basket bed for him to ride back to Knoxville in. I kept my hand on his little feet all the way. Seven pounds, nine ounces -- oh, how precious! I could hardly wait to call Mom and tell them to get there as quick as they could, but no one was home when I called her! I called Don and told him I was home with our baby. He got mixed up and told his daddy that the baby weighed nine ounces. Don's father said, "What's wrong with this baby? Is it premature?"

That night, needless to say, we had lots of company. Mom and the girls were on their way to my house when I had called. Oh, I was sitting on the bed holding him when they came in. He had started to cry a little bit, and I thought he needed a dry diaper. When I pulled the diaper off, Mama scared me to death. "Oh Lord!" she shouted.

Then I said, "What's wrong with my baby?"

"His bottom is red as can be!" So I caked him with Vaseline and put on a new diaper. I fed him a pre-mixed bottle, and each of the girls had to hold the bottle, then they had to hold the baby. Mama was scared to death. She could hardly hold him herself, she was so scared. "Oh, girls, we have to be careful. His head is so soft!"

They couldn't keep their hands off of him. "Oh Margie, we're aunts! We're aunts!"

"Guess what! I'm a mother!" I said.

Chapter 23

Don and I were still living in our Shenandoah apartment at that time, but God provides. "Thank you, Jehovah Jira," I prayed when Mr. Mulindore called to say our new home would be finished in about eight weeks. When David was nine weeks old, we moved into our little new house. It had a little entrance hall with a coat closet. You could go to the left and go to the bedrooms, or you could go to the right and go to the living room. The kitchen was big enough to put our table in it. The house had three bedrooms and a bath and a half.

Pam and Judy said, "This will be our bedroom," about the room that was next to David's nursery.

Don said, "I'm sorry, but it will be our den for a little while."

"That's fine. We will sleep on the couch," they said.

I had carpet and a dishwasher. It wasn't long until Mom had carpet and dishwasher, too. David slept like a little lamb. I even had to set the alarm clock to wake me up to give him a bottle in the middle of the night. I asked the doctor, "Are you sure nothing's wrong with him?" "You are going to make me pull my hair out!" he said. "Don't you know that all the other mothers say, 'Can't you make my baby sleep more?'"

My Sunday school class gave me a shower when David was two weeks old. They gave me the cutest little boy clothes for him to wear to Sunday school, and lots of little one piece sleepers. I thought that was wonderful. One piece! I didn't have to worry about matching everything. I pinned his socks to each Sunday outfit so I would know which pair matched. He was a thumb-sucker, but I kept on 'til I had him suck his pacifier instead of his thumb, because I was afraid I wouldn't be able to get him to stop sucking his thumb when he was bigger. I could take the pacifier away. Oh my David! He was a doll baby!

When David was about six months old, he dropped his pacifier. He was squalling, and I couldn't find it. So I was going to call someone to come and find it for me. I put him down in the floor, and just a minute later, I heard him sucking on the pacifier! So from then on, I just let him find it himself when he dropped anything.

Boy, he loved that infant feeder. He would gobble up a jar of baby food before I could say scat! At about seven months old, when I would lay him on the blanket, he would start scooting on his tummy. One day, he scooted right off that blanket and went almost crawling.

I'll never forget the day I lost him. I put his little clothes on and put him on the floor so that he could get some exercise. This was before he learned to walk. I was talking on the phone, and he was rolling around on the floor right beside me. I talked and talked, and in a minute, I didn't hear him. "Oh Judy, wait a minute. I don't hear David." I walked down the hall, and I looked under his baby bed. I couldn't find him. Just as I was about to get off the phone to call someone to help, I found him asleep in the bathroom on an orange foam rubber foot that was in front of the bathtub. I never lost him again, because he would always go to that foam rubber foot. Needless to say, his favorite color was "owange." I also put bells on his sleepers and on his shoes when he learned to walk.

Well, he was almost crawling, but he kept laying his cheek on the floor, and I wondered if his head was too heavy for him to lift up. By then I had met some friends on Ada Lane where our new house was. My friend had a little girl about six months older than David, and another little girl about eleven months older than that. Her name was Sherrie McCarter. I asked her what she thought about David crawling. She said, "Oh, he's just doing his own thing. He'll get up and walk soon."

When he was nine months old, I would put his little shoes on and his coat, and I'd say, "Let's go to the mailbox." I would hold his little hands, and he would walk to the mailbox with me holding his hands. He would stop right there at the mailbox.

One day, my friend Cartha Lynn said, "Can't he walk by himself yet?"

"Oh, I think he could, but he won't," I said.

"Let me see if I can help him."

"What are you going to do?"

"Well, don't act like you think I might hurt your baby," she said.

"Well, I'm over-protective." I said.

"You didn't have to tell me that. Now you get at the end of the hall by the bedroom door, and I'll get up by the kitchen door."

She put David on the floor in front of her. He was saying, "Mama, Mama!"

"Walk to Mama," she said. He cried. And she kept saying, "Walk to Mama." All of a sudden he was mad, and he ran right down the hall to me.

"There you go," she said. From then on, he was able to walk by himself. When David was two years old, he climbed on my lap, and put his little arms around me. Oh, how blessed I felt. Then he said, "Mommy, I know how to 'wuv' you with my arms, but I don't know how to 'wuv' Jesus."

"You love Jesus in your heart," I said. "Would you like Mommy to take you to the book store and buy a Bible for little boys?"

"Humm," he said. And that meant 'yes.' So we went to Evangel Bookstore. The people there thought he was a doll baby.

They said, "Let him down. We'll watch him for you." So I set him down, and they took him back to the sticker pictures. He loved them! So I talked to the lady about a Bible that would have pictures in a book and a record to go with it.

I said, "You must have one, because I've prayed about it, and this is where God sent me to find it."

"Yes, we have only one."

"Oh, thank You, Lord," I said. David had all these picture books that had a record with them, and the record would say 'ding' when it was time to turn the page, and I wanted David to have a Bible that would do that. I still have his little Bible. It was called <u>The Bible in Pictures for Little Eyes</u>. It took several little discs to make the children's Bible. Every morning when I would get the dishes washed, and it was time for juice, we would have refreshments together. He would sit on my lap, and we would listen to the records and turn the picture pages. I am still thanking God for <u>The Bible in Pictures for Little Eyes</u>. It had music in the background, and when I put on the first record, David started to cry. He said, "That 'wecord' 'scawes' me."

"It's just music," I said.

"But it 'scawes' me." So we went on to the second record, and David learned more about God and Jesus. Everyday we read that Bible together, and sometimes at night we did a repeat.

Chapter 24

I love telling things that David said when he was little. One day we were at McDonalds. David was almost three. Sherrie said, "David, if you and Lisa throw a fry or two out to the birds, they will come down and get them." There was a bunch of pigeons there. They threw out some fries and immediately, down came the pigeons.

Lisa and David clapped their hands and laughed. "Oh Mommy!" he said. "I love the birdies!"

"How do you know you love the birds?" I said.

"I know I love the birds, Mommy!"

"Well, you love them with your heart, and now you will know how to love Jesus with your heart."

"Oh, Mommy! Now I know how to love Jesus with my heart!"

The next year when he was three, it was around Easter time. He had three Bibles spread out in his room in the floor. He had <u>The Bible in Pictures for Little Eyes</u>, another beginner Bible, and a junior Bible. They all had pictures. He kept turning pages and trying to find the same thing in each Bible. All of a sudden, I heard him scream.

Oh, Lord, I thought, and I hurried as fast as I could to his room, which was next to the kitchen. He was lying with his face in the junior Bible. "Oh, Mommy, Mommy!" he cried.

"What, angel? What's wrong?"

"Is this Jesus on this cross? Is this the Baby Jesus on this cross?" This should have taught me to tell all, for I had saved this story to tell him when he was older.

"Well, darling, He wasn't a baby when He was on the cross."

"Was He a man like my daddy?"

"Yes, He was." David cried and cried.

"Why are you crying, Mommy?" I was crying because Christ had died on the cross for our sins. He had given us this precious gift, and He had blessed me with this baby boy. "Oh, I want to tell someone about Jesus," David said. "Who do we know, Mommy?"

"Well, let me think." Before I could think about someone who didn't know Jesus, he said, "I want to dig, and dig, and dig, and find that devil that did this to Jesus."

I said, "Jesus didn't have to die on the cross, but He wanted to do it for us."

"When I grow up," David said, "I will tell lots of people about Jesus." He kept reminding me of that all through school. As a teenager, he went up at Central Baptist Church Fountain City and said that he had been called to become a minister.

That same year that David found out that Jesus died on the cross, Don decided we should go to Birmingham, Alabama, to visit his sister, Jane. We had visited her once before, and I felt uneasy while we were there, as if we weren't wanted. That was before David was born. Jana, Jane's baby was crawling at the time, and Don's mother had warned, "Don't go down there and step on the baby!" Sure enough, Don did. This trip, Jane had two children, Jana and Will, and we had David.

After one afternoon and one morning at Jane's, she came in and announced we could do whatever we wanted to do, but they were going to a bowling tournament. They said we could stay there or catch the bus home. I said we wanted to leave. Don asked them how long they'd be gone, and they said, "Three or four days." On the way home, I decided that was our last visit to Jane's house.

On the trip home, the bus stopped in Chattanooga. At the bus station there, I had one of my scariest experiences as a mother. I had nightmares about it for a week. Don had decided we should get off at the rest stop and stretch since we had been riding for quite a while. He said we'd get a snack. We got off and on our way across the street a woman came up behind us. The woman said, "This is a good one, this is a good one. I found one. Quack, quack" I said, "Do you work here?" "No," she said, "I just try to help people along. I'll show you where the vending machines are. Hello! I just love little boys like you. Can I pick you up?" she asked David. "Can she pick me up?" he innocently asked me. "No, David." "Why not?" "Because she's a stranger."

David and I went to sit down. He asked to get down, so I gave in. As always, I had bells on his shoes so I could hear him. Of course, Don was with us, too. Then I heard, "Quack, quack. Quack, quack. This is a good one, this is a good one." She was very loud this time. It scared me, so I said, "David, come here!" "Here I am, Mommy." I picked him up and put him on my lap. The strange lady continued talking: "I would love to take you home with me. I have lots of toys at my house. Would you like to come home with me." "Can I come home with her?" David asked. "Quack, quack." "Please don't do that, you scare me!" I pleaded. Don then got up and announced he had to go to the bathroom. "Don't go to the bathroom!" I said, but off he went. I then heard a man's voice saying, "What's wrong? Do you need help?" A man at the bus station had come over and asked if she was bothering me. He told me not to worry about her, that she was there all the time and that she scared someone with a little girl last week. The man then hollered, "Get away from them!" Don returned from bathroom and we went on our way to the bus.

When he was about three and half, David told me, "I want some juice, 'owange' juice." I reached into the refrigerator. "I don't think we have any."

"Oh, yes, we have some, Mommy." I couldn't find it. "Pick up me!" he said. I picked him up in one arm, and he took my other arm in his hands and guided it to find the orange juice. "Thank you, David. You just used your eyes to help Mommy."

"I liked it," he said.

"Me, too," I said.

One day when it was almost time for his fourth birthday, I heard him in his room. He was lying on his bed saying, "pig-let," over and over again. Then I heard him say, "Aunt L-iz." He came running into my room. "Mommy! Mommy," he said. "I got you birthday present." My birthday was May 2nd, and his was May 16th.

"What is it?" I asked, as I hugged him up in my arms. "It's 'pig-let'." "So, what's different about 'pig-let'?" "Mommy, I'm giving you my L." "Can you say 'look'?" And he said, "Look!" "Can you say 'listen'?" And he said, "Listen! Mommy, Mommy, call Aunt Liz on the phone!" So I called Liz, our dear friend, on the phone. She answered and said, "How are you, Margie?"

"I'm great. David has a present for you."

"Is it her birthday?" David asked.

"Liz, it is an un-birthday present!" She laughed, and I handed the phone to David.

"Say 'hello, Aunt Liz'," and he did. Liz laughed and clapped and was as happy about those L's as we were. He did the same our next birthday with his R's. I knew that child was going to be very intelligent. I mean, what other baby gives you his letters for your birthday?

Chapter 25

When David was about seven, I started having headaches. My legs hurt often, too. It seemed that I had a really hard time keeping everything done I needed to do. My hair needed to look beautiful all the time, the house needed to look great, the meals needed to be cook, clothes needed to be washed, I needed to have programs ready for G.A. group, R.A. group, Wednesday night prayer services, Saturday night banquet, and a church service for any Sunday. My David, that sweet boy, was so good. He entertained himself and never caused me a minute's worry about where he was or what he was into. I tried leaving a Sunday open now and then, just to give myself some recuperating time, but I felt guilty when I did. I promised God that, if He let me walk, I would give my legs in service to Him, and that's exactly what I intended to do.

Just before David was born, I made my second gospel record. We titled it <u>By Request</u>. It was recorded at Broadway Baptist Church. We were able to use their magnificent pipe organ, and the instrumentals sounded much better on this album. When David was three, I made <u>Double Blessings</u>, and when he was about five, I made <u>The Lord Has Given Me a Song</u>. From the time I left Carson Newman until David was about eight years old, I went to churches all over the country, just teaching and telling my story about what Jesus has done for me and what He can do for you. I loved the evangelistic time in my life.

I always wanted to talk the talk and walk the walk. If I said I was going to do something, I was going to do it. God is so good. Before David was born, I had thought I wanted a little girl. But after I got my boy, I wouldn't have swapped him for a dozen girls – but I would have taken them in addition to him! Somehow, my sweet boy got it into his mind that I would have rather had a girl. I loved on him and told him over and over, "That's before I had a boy that I thought I wanted a girl. I wouldn't swap you for any girl!", but I think he chose not to believe me. One day, when he was about 9 or 10, he was reading his Bible. He came to me and said, "Mom, a son is better than a daughter. The Bible says so." Everybody wanted sons. "So do I!" I said. "My darling, please believe me. I am glad to have a son. See, God knows what is better for us than we do, and He knew I needed a son." At 18, I took him shopping, and he told the girl in the store that I wanted a girl, but I got stuck with him. So sometimes, no matter how hard we try, our kids just don't hear us. God let him know, somehow, that I know I was blessed when He gave me my son.

David continued to grow "in wisdom and in stature and in favor with God and man." He was a blessing all throughout his adolescence and brought me more joy than I could have imagined. He is now the pastor of a Presbyterian church in Mobile, Alabama. His wife's name is Rosalyn, and her parents are from China. She has her doctorate in music. She teaches at two colleges there and does worldwide concerts on the piano. She and David have two little boys named Joseph and Daniel. Thank you, God, for my David.

Chapter 26

The headaches grew worse with Don's temper tantrums. At that time, we separated for a while. I decided to leave and tell Don when he came home that night to get his clothes and go somewhere else so I could come back home. I had a friend named Laverne Humphries. She was president of the Association for the Blind in Knoxville and had remained my friend throughout the years. I called her and asked, "Laverne, can I come over to the association to stay for a night or two? "Sure," she said, "You and David can come on over to my house." It was a wonderful haven. David and I were glad to relax and not have to worry about a temper for a night or two. Toni, Laverne's foster sister, came down and cooked dinner that night. I just fell in love with that energetic young lady. Her little girl was about two years old, and like her name, was a Joy. Toni was the best young mother I had bumped into in a while. She never yelled at Joy. When she would tell Joy to sit on the couch, she was getting up walking toward the couch and sitting Joy down. I thought that was fabulous. Joy knew to mind because Toni was a mover. I watched it work for the next few years. As Joy got bigger, all Toni had to say was "Joy do this" and Joy would do it.

Toni worked for Laverne at the Association. They took David to school those few days I spent the night there and took me to pick him up. I learned that they had a Braille switchboard at the shop. I was lonely since David had started to school. "Laverne," I begged, "Let me try and work the switchboard." "OK," she said, "Go up and tell Edna you want to try." I had learned the switchboard in Talladega. "I don't know how a blind person can work it," she said. "Why not?" "Well, go up and look at it and tell me what you think." I checked it out, and discovered it wasn't Brailled. They were just running the probe on the finger over the lights. When they found the call that was coming in, they had to count the lights to know where to plug it in. It was nigh on to impossible without the Braille. I saw it in my mind, exactly how the board was brailed in Talladega. I went down and told Laverne, "I can Brailled this board for you." "I don't know," she said. "Please let me do this for you. I can help." Toni spoke up: "Why don't you let her?" "Oh, OK, who cares. Go ahead. Braille it, if you can." I was excited. "Come on, Toni, get some labeling tape." "OK," she said, and up the stairs we went. "OK, Edna," we said when we arrived, "We're going to be Brailling your board. We'll try to stay out of your way." "OK," she responded. "I don't know Braille myself, but it will help Bruce at night when he's in here trying to take the calls." *It will help me if I get to work one of the shifts myself,* I thought.

I got a call from Don that night informing he was going over to his parents' house to stay, so I went back home to my little house on Ada Lane. David felt frightened with Don being gone. He said,

"My light's already off, Mom." But when I touched it the switch was up. I can tell when the light is on or off by the position of the switch. When I turned it off, he said, "Don't turn the light on, Mom. I can't sleep. You can't see, Mommy, and I can. I know when the light is on and off." "Are you afraid?" I asked. "No, Mommy, I just want you to leave the light off, just like I had it." "OK, I'll leave the light on." "It's off!" "OK, Dave, I won't bother the light. Now, go to sleep." On Sunday afternoon, Toni and Ron, her husband, drove over to see how David and I were doing. They found us doing fine.

I started working the switchboard on Monday morning. I was having more headaches and the pain was getting worse all over me. Laverne said they would take me to therapy if I needed them to. That's when I started seeing Dr. Frye. Toni and I were getting to know each other more and more every day. Toni would come to get me from therapy. "What did Dr. Frye say today, Margie?" And I would tell her what we talked about and what Dr. Frye had said. I found her applying Dr. Frye's advice to her own situations. "I like this -- I'm getting therapy, too," she said. Laverne didn't like the fact that we were getting close. She was jealous. She loved us, but she didn't want us to be that close. So she quit letting Toni take me to therapy. She sent Paul, the regular transportation person, to take me there. Toni called me at night after I was home from the switchboard to hear what Dr. Frye had said that day.

Toni started telling me about her problems and how she didn't have enough time for Ron and Joy because she had to cook and clean for Laverne and her mom. By the time she got to her own home she was worn out. Laverne was supposed to be making Toni's house payments, but she let them slide. All of a sudden, Toni was afraid she was going to lose her home. She asked for my advice. *Well, here I go*, I thought. "I think you should find a job somewhere else and take in your own money and make your own house payment. You're letting her have your responsibility and you are taking on part of hers." There were other problems we talked over, and we learned to love each other so much. She felt like a sister. I was surprised when Toni took my advice and got a job at a local childcare center. She was nervous at first but found herself fitting in very well after a while. Laverne was really mad at her.

Meanwhile, I kept working the switchboard. I worked for about three months. The first two or three weeks Laverne gave me money. After that, she said she didn't have it and would I mind waiting. After three or four months I decided to quit since I wasn't getting any money for it. It wasn't long until Laverne called and asked me if I would be in a play. The association could get money if they would get blind people to put on a play. It would be considered an extra program for the year. It was summertime, and David was home from school, and it would get us out of the house. I really had fun. The play we did was "The Glass Menagerie", and I played Laura. It turned out really well.

Chapter 27

1979 was declared "The Year of the Child," and the next year brought "Kelly doll" into our lives. Dr. Frye sent me to Dr. Kristi Hurst, a primary care physician. She was the sweetest lady. Mom said she had the biggest blue eyes she had ever seen. She gave me the Lupus test, thinking I might have Lupus because I had so much pain. She tested for three other conditions, but I don't remember what they were. I told her, "Oh, my face even hurts." She said, "It doesn't look like it hurts." That made me mad. I told her I didn't care what it looked like, but I knew what it felt like. So they put me on Darvacet for pain and ativan for anxiety. When I went to therapy, I asked Dr. Frye why they were giving me something for my nerves. "This pain is not in my head; it is all over me and I didn't just dream it up." "We are trying to relax you, Margie, so maybe you won't hurt as much if you are relaxed." The orthopedic doctor put me on Naprosen.

Soon after, I went to East Tennessee Children's Rehabilitation Center where I met Kelly. I had a dream about her before I met her. God had sent me my special little girl and I knew it the moment I saw her. When they introduced us, I loved her immediately. Volunteering my time with Kelly got my mind off the pain more than anything else. The teacher named the class the Vital Class because certainly it was vital for these children. Some had wonderful parents while others, like little Tricia, had been abused. Kelly was the baby of the class. As summer approached, Kelly's mom asked me if I would babysit Kelly for the summer. I came home and asked Dave, "What would you think about you and me babysitting a little blind girl for the summer?" "What would we do with her?" he asked. "We could teach her how to walk and feed herself and say some words. She can't even hold her bottle yet, Dave." "OK, Mom, I'll help you with her." And so we did it. The first word she learned to say was "Day" for David.

The following section about Kelly was written by me many years ago:

Kelly's Song

It is more blessed to give than to receive.

My heart was joyous, as I explained to my young son, David, how we would teach baby Kelly to reach out for things and help her learn to play and talk. We would find new things to fill her days, so she would want to stay awake except for naptime.

My excitement was catching, and David asked, "Oh, Mother, what else will we teach her?"

"If she can learn to chew, we can teach her to eat table food," I answered.

"It will be a fun summer, won't it, Mother?"

"Yes, oh, yes it will!"

"I know I will love her. When can I see her?" he asked.

"Tomorrow at the picnic," I told him. We clapped our hands thinking about the school picnic the next day at East Tennesee Rehabilitation. We could hardly wait for Monday of the next week, when we would start working with Kelly.

That conversation had taken place over twelve months ago. I lay awake one night thinking about the year that had just passed and how I had come to the decision to keep the little girl. I had been working with her and loving her since I held her on the first day I went with Debbie to be a volunteer helper in Marsha's and Debbie's classroom for preschool blind children.

When I arrived, Marsha let me get to know each of the little children one by one. I loved them all immediately.

Marsha said, "The baby of the class isn't here, yet." At that same moment, the door opened. In her joyful and unique way, she announced, "Here's Kelly!"

She greeted the little one with, "There's someone here who wants to meet you."

Then back to me, "This is our baby."

My arms automatically reached out to Kelly.

Her mother warned, "She will cry."

When I assured her that I didn't mind, her quiet, gentle mother sat her on my lap.

To my delight, Kelly didn't cry. I hugged her close to me and told her how glad I felt that she let me hold her. As her little hand reached up to my face, I answered her touch with, "Sweet, sweet baby, I love you." Then I sang to her and played with her in the same way I would any other baby. Suddenly, she was laughing out loud!

Marsha, Debbie, and Kelly's mother asked excitedly, "Did Kelly laugh?"

"Well, yes, she did," I answered, puzzled at what sounded like amazement in their voices.

The long silence was electric. I thought I heard both sobs and laughter, but I couldn't tell from whom. "What's the matter?"

"We've had her how long, now?"

"I don't know. Months."

Marsha and Debbie were talking at once. "What a surprise!" one of them nearly shouted.

"What?" I begged, still bewildered.

"It's just that..." Her mother's soft voice was weak and broken. She sniffed and took a deep breath. "It's just that Kelly has never laughed before."

The only expression I could find for my shock was to hug this tiny person on my lap even closer. Surprise, I thought, as I pressed her to me. That's no surprise. It's a miracle!

After class was over, Marsha told me I had helped a lot, and asked if I would come again the next week. I went each Monday from the first of March until the end of May. I had been praying every day that somehow God would let me continue helping Kelly.

As I was feeling sad because I wouldn't be seeing her during the next few months, God showed me the way. Her mother asked if I would be interested in keeping her little girl that summer, so she could work at a children's camp. I didn't have to think! I knew it was the answer to my prayer.

I had learned during the time I was working with Kelly that she had been born four months prematurely, weighing only 1½ pounds. Her stay in an isolette was extensive and open-heart surgery when she was only a few days old added to the trauma. When she was finally able to go home, her mother became concerned about her eyes and soon learned that she was blind.

Marsha wondered why Kelly had responded so well when I worked and played with her. Was it because she had somehow realized that I was working with only the same four senses she was? I wasn't sure why Kelly had reacted so well to me. I just knew I loved her desperately, and I couldn't wait to help her catch up to her age level.

As I dropped off to sleep, I was glad I had accepted the invitation to participate in the celebration of "The Year of the Child." That was when I had first met Marsha and Debbie. During this autumn celebration, Marsha and Debbie came walking through the big mall with three of the children from their class.

"What is here?" I heard a little girl ask.

"This is a lady with her dummy, and look, Deana, she reads Braille like you do."

"Is your little girl blind?" I asked.

"She is my student," Marsha said, excitedly.

"Where do you teach?" I asked.

"I teach a class for preschool blind children."

"Oh, how wonderful!" I exclaimed. "How I'd love to be a part of all that!"

"If I ever need a volunteer, I'll let you know, and you can come work with us." But my work in the classroom didn't begin until March 1.

Its June now, and my summer with Kelly had begun. The air was filled with excitement, challenge, joy and fun. Keeping that little girl awake during the day, so she could sleep at night was my first big challenge. If I sat her down for one minute, she would be asleep. Sometimes even when I was playing with her, she would fall asleep. I had learned from Marsha and Debbie that finding the thing a child is most interested in is the first step toward helping her. I kept searching for Kelly's interest. Sleeping seemed to be it, and that would never do. If I would sing songs, "Mary Had a Little Lamb," "The Three Little Kittens," "Jack Horner," and other nursery rhymes, she would sit in her highchair and let me feed her. If I just talked, she would cry and close those lips tight.

On Friday, it hit me! Music is her "thing"! I made a tape of nursery rhyme songs and set the recorder under her baby bed. "Now, Kelly, you can play in your bed and listen to the music," I told her. And she did just that.

Fran, her mother, came in as she had done for the past week, to ask if Kelly had stayed awake longer today. "Yes, come and see," I said, as we went into Kelly's room. When she saw Kelly standing in her baby bed, bouncing up and down, keeping time with the music, she mused, "I was beginning to worry about her. But she can do anything, if she really wants to."

Standing in her bed, pulling up to the chair or standing on her feet and hands, bouncing her bottom up and down, while the music played was one thing. If I said, "Come on, Kelly, let's walk," that was a different story. She would not stand up for anything, and I would have to find a way to make her stand. I would put my hands under her arms and lift her body up to the right height for standing. Instead of putting her feet on the floor, she would swing those little legs toward me and around my waist they would go. At the same time, her arms would go around my neck.

One day, I scooted close to the wall in the hall where we were struggling with this task. I positioned my legs Indian-style on the floor and placed Kelly with her back against the wall. Screaming at the top of her lungs, she hung onto my neck, and I slid my hands down to straighten her legs to a standing position. I moved a little closer and raised my knees just high enough to put them against her legs, so she couldn't bend them, as she usually did. Then she bent over from the hips and put her arms around me and held on tight. To stop her screaming, I started singing, "Mary Had a Little Lamb".

She quieted, and I slowly moved her back against the wall, and somehow got her wrists into my hands. I clapped her hands for her and sang for ten minutes. She was standing because I wanted her to stand, and she knew it. It had been a battle of wills, and I had won.

An hour later, we did this again, but this time there was no screaming, because I sang from the beginning. Five times a day for ten minutes, we practiced this technique. "You have to learn to walk," I told her. "You might be too heavy for me to carry next summer."

"Hold your bottle, Kelly," I urged, as she stiffened her little arms and straightened her fingers to show me that we were definitely in battle again. When I would put her hands on the bottle, she would let go of the nipple and cry with all her lung power. David would come running to see what the matter was. One day he asked, "Was I ever afraid to hold my bottle, Mama?"

"No," I answered, "but sometimes, you would get lazy if you were sleepy."

"Did I pull my hands away like that?"

"You just folded your little hands under your chin and said, 'Mama' in a sleepy tone."

"Did you hold it for me or not?"

"Yes, I did," I said.

"Then, hold it for Kelly," he ordered.

"When she learns to hold it for herself, then I will hold it for her sometimes." I wondered why he had felt that she was afraid instead of just being stubborn.

That night, a friend called to ask about Kelly's day. I told her about the "battle of the bottle," as she and I referred to each new thing I began with Kelly. I heard her catch her breath sharply. I asked, "What is it?"

"It's the dream."

"Which dream?" I asked.

"The one you had a year ago in March about the baby."

Then it was my turn to feel the strangeness one feels when they say, "It feels like I have dreamed this before," only greater. Because I really knew I had dreamed about Kelly before I ever knew her—before she was born. "I remember," I said.

In my dream, the doorbell rang during the night, and someone said to wait five minutes and then bring in the banana box he was leaving on the porch. David, Don and I let the five minutes pass, and my husband opened the door and lifted the banana box into the house.

David peeked through the handle opening in the box and said, "It's a baby, Mama! It's so still, I think its dead."

"Oh, no!" I cried out, as the dream went on.

"It's okay, Mama, it just wiggled a toe."

I opened the box and lifted the little girl up and held her close to me. She lay so still. Then I heard that same loud cry that I had experienced that very day. David handed me a bottle from the box. I put the nipple in her mouth, and she sucked hungrily. But when I tried to put her hands around the bottle, she let go of the nipple to yell and pull her hands away.

"She doesn't want the bottle," I said.

"Yes, she does, Mama," David told me. "She wants you to hold it for her."

"Oh, Allison," I breathed, as reality called me back from my dream. "What do you think it means?"

We said simultaneously in a question, "God?"

It was mid-July, as I sat in the redwood swing holding the sleeping child. The swing was sheltered on one side by the back of my yellow house, and on the other side there was an oak tree for shade. As she slept, her legs and arms moved slowly, until she was lying in a fetal position. I swung and Kelly slept. My heart ached, and I wished I didn't love her so much. Tears wet my cheeks, and for the first time, I could understand in a very small way some of the hurt any mother with a special child must feel.

At the beginning of the summer, the big questions had been, "Is anything wrong with Kelly besides her eyes? No," I had quickly told myself. Now, I wondered if I could believe my own deep down feeling of love and hope that Kelly would respond, learn and have a life of fulfillment.

Three days ago, I had been glad when Fran asked how I would feel about taking Kelly for an evaluation to see how she was improving, physically and developmentally. I wanted to learn as much as I could about Kelly so I could help her more.

"It will make it easier for me," she said, "and you can tell me whatever they say."

There we were the next morning, Kelly and I, sitting in a small room, listening and talking with the psychologist. Kelly felt my tension and sat with her face hidden against me.

"So, this is the baby you are keeping this summer," the psychologist mused.

"Yes, I love her so much."

"On what level do you feel she is functioning?" he questioned.

"Well," I ventured, "maybe about ten months old."

"All right, let's find out. Do you know why her head has a square shape?"

"Oh," I said, "that's probably because she had to lie on her back so long in the isolette."

"It could be something else," he said quietly.

"What?"

"Oh, it may not," he said, but the question had been left for me to ponder. "Does she demand her rights?" he asked.

"I don't know what you mean." I was beginning to feel confused.

"Does she cry when she is holding something and you try to take it from her?"

"No."

"Does she pull up in her bed?"

"Sure," I said.

"Does she walk around it?"

"I'm, um, not sure," I stammered.

"Does she eat table food well?"

"We are working on that now," I told him.

"Working? How?"

"Well, I'm trying to help her learn to chew."

"That comes naturally," he said almost sharply.

I felt my head start to ache.

"Does she have a favorite toy?"

"Uh . . ."

"What about a blanket or something soft, or something to suck?"

"No, but . . ." Now my heart was pounding along with my head. "She likes music and can keep time with it, and she puts her face in the water and kicks her legs and arms. She is staying awake more every day," I blurted out in one breath.

"You are getting closer to this child that you should," he told me.

I was getting angry. *Who did he think he was?* I thought.

"Is she getting attached to you?"

"What do you mean?" I asked. "How would I know?"

"Well," he said, "does she cry for you when her mother comes to get her at night?"

"No, she is a good baby," I answered in Kelly's behalf. "She doesn't cry when her mother leaves her, either."

"I see," the psychologist said, as if he had just learned something I was unaware of. "Does she try to hold her spoon?"

"Well, no, but she is learning to hold her bottle," I said shakily.

"May I take her now and see what she will do for me?"

"Sure," I said, and handed Kelly to him reluctantly.

Of course, he was kind and gentle with her. Still, Kelly wasn't cooperative. When she was back on my lap again, she put one leg on each side of me and hid her face against me, as usual.

"Do you know why she hides her face?"

"I think her eyes hurt. She has some glaucoma."

The psychologist offered me his theory. "I think it is because she is insecure. Turn around so I can watch her expression, please."

I turned Kelly around and, as the conversation continued, the psychologist observed, "She's asleep."

"No, she isn't."

"I can see her, and she is."

"I am holding her, and I know her, and when she goes to sleep, she puts her head down, and she isn't breathing the way she breathes when she sleeps," I argued.

"Now, she is awake," he said.

"I know I can't see," I protested, "but I know when a baby is sleeping, especially when she is on my lap."

"There she goes again," he said.

"What?" I asked, not understanding.

"There is a blank expression on her face, as if she is sleeping. Now, it is gone."

Suddenly, my anger turned to fear. "Do you think she is having light seizures?"

Hearing the alarm in my voice, he answered, "I did not say that."

"This must be what Sherrie and Laurie see when they think she is asleep, and I know that she isn't," I confessed.

"Does she hear well?" he asked.

"I think so."

"When the blank look comes on her face again, I will... She's doing it now! Try to get her attention. Call her name."

"Kelly, Kelly!" I said.

"Shake her a little," he told me. "There, it is gone. I will slap a book down on the desk the next time. You make sure that you don't jump."

"I'll try not," I said.

"OK. Here goes."

He slammed a book down with a bang, and Kelly never made a move. I jumped, even though I tried not to. He blew a whistle. Kelly didn't jump.

"What does this mean," I asked her.

"I'm not sure. I will bring in the speech and hearing person."

The speech and hearing specialist came in, took Kelly on her lap and clicked her high-heeled shoes on the floor. "Yes, she can hear."

They whispered something about her reflexes, and then went outside the door. Next, the medical doctor took his turn. I heard the psychologist say to the girl who would take Kelly and me to the next office, "Let her carry Kelly. I want to watch and see how she manages."

I didn't have to worry about doing that; I was in good practice. I stood up with Kelly and her legs went around my waist as usual, and I put one arm around her and held to the girl's arm with my other hand. I could feel their eyes watching me, as we went down the hall to the other office.

"I will examine Kelly, if you have time," the medical doctor informed me.

"That's why I'm here," I said.

"What are these scars on her neck? They look like surgical scars."

"They had to feed her protein in the isolette."

"How long was she in the isolette, and how long did they have to feed her through her neck?"

"I don't know," I answered.

"You are keeping her without knowing any of her medical history," he growled at me. "What's wrong with her heart?"

"I can't remember."

"What are you doing with this baby? Her mother should have brought her," he said much too loudly.

"I don't know why you are angry with me," I said. "Her mother trusts me, and I was glad to bring her."

"You don't need to keep this baby. Anything could happen to her, and you wouldn't even know it."

"I am not dumb," I said, "just blind, and I certainly would know if anything was happening to her."

"She has many problems, and a blind person shouldn't keep her."

If I hadn't been a Christian, I would have lost my temper.

"Let her mother introduce her to new foods."

"Why? She wants me to help with her learning how to chew."

"Something isn't right with her mouth and throat, and she may never learn to chew. You may let her choke to death."

"I promise I would know if she were choking."

"She has an infected throat and red ears. She will have a high fever tomorrow. Tell her mother you can't keep her if she's sick. She could die you know," the doctor said bluntly, as he went out the door and closed it with a bang.

Kelly and I were then taken back to the waiting room where I sat shaking. I felt the doctor hated me for being blind, and I could have hated him for being so ignorant in his knowledge about how much or how little being blind has to do with what you know or don't know, or what you can or can't do.

The psychologist finally came back and told me she was sorry, but they wouldn't be able to tell me anything they had found out because I was not Kelly's mother.

"I just want to ask you one question," I said, "what is her developmental level? You see, I am trying to teach her some new things that she is behind in."

"I wouldn't try too hard," she said, "just let her pick up whatever she will."

"What are you saying?" I asked, thinking this is incredible.

"To find out where a child is developmentally, you have to separate the motor skills from other things it knows."

"Oh," I said, realizing almost everything that Kelly did was considered a motor skill.

"I'm sorry," she repeated.

"If you are telling me Kelly can't learn, you're wrong."

"When a child is this far behind, they usually don't catch up."

"She will!" I declared.

"You are too attached to this baby," she told me.

"Well, what will I tell her mother?"

"Tell her to call us."

I was glad to leave, and so was Kelly. Loretta had come to pick us up, and I told her all about what had happened. "Now what will you do?" she asked.

"I'll feed her with an infant feeder, until I decide what is right."

"And what if she really is getting sick?"

"Oh, Loretta, I hurt as if she were mine. I love her so much, and I want to catch her up, and now... oh, Kelly, Kelly," I cried.

My thoughts turned from this memory, as I kept swinging. "Oh, dear God, help me to know how to help this little child who has become so special to me and to all who know and love her. If she can learn, Lord, show me some response from her. Please, oh, please, God."

At that moment, Kelly moved. She stretched her arms and legs. She stretched her arms above her head as far as they would reach and her legs as far as they would reach.

"Kelly," I said, "what are you doing?"

"Hi-yi-yi, ry-ry-ry."

She had never stretched so far and that was the first vocal response, except for a laugh or a cry, I had ever heard from Kelly.

"Thank You, God. Oh, thank You," I said. The tears now were of pure joy and gratitude. "Now we know you will learn! We will go full speed ahead for the rest of the summer!"

By the end of the summer, Kelly not only held her bottle while eating, she even played with it. I held her hands while she walked down the hall to meet her mother.

Loretta came to see her the last day I kept her that summer. I was so proud of all she had learned. "Loretta, listen to Kelly's song."

"O.K.," she said, excitedly. "Sing!"

I began, "Hi-yi-yi." Kelly echoed me, "Hi-yi-yi."

I sang, "Ry-ry-ry."

Again, Kelly followed, "Ry-ry-ry."

I sang, "This is Kelly's song," and we went through the whole thing again.

Loretta clapped and exclaimed, "Oh, Kelly, you did so well!"

We heard a car drive up, and I said, "Oh, Loretta, you will finally get to meet Fran."

Instead, Kelly's grandmother came in and said, "Fran sent me to get Kelly today. I told her I didn't have a car seat, and she said that I could just put her in a banana box and fasten the seat belt around her."

Loretta and I exchanged glances of amazement, as the dream flashed through both our minds. Neither of us had to say a word. My heart was filled with joy and gratitude. "Thank You, God, for answering prayer."

Kelly is almost five now, and her three-day visit with us this summer brought much joy to Don, David, and me. Kelly said things like, "Hey, Margie, want to go swing? My new shoes are spiffy. I can open the door. Let's find the table and my bib, it's time to eat."

"What would you like for lunch?" I asked her.

"I like something Italian, with hot sauce and cold slaw. I like banana pudding for dessert."

She could count to twenty, sing part of her ABC's, say her prayers, and, oh, yes -- no more diapers!

UPDATE:

Kelly celebrated her 30th birthday on November 28, 2008. She is a high school graduate, has taken several years of voice lessons where she learned to sing in German and Italian. A man took an interest in her and gave her an organ. Her grandmother Inza had already worked with her on the piano, and she could play many songs. Kelly made it seem easy to slide into playing the organ and using the techniques needed for that. Oh, how I love that young lady who was once my baby. I tell Kelly she was my heart child. She wishes Billy and I would move to Knoxville and let her live with us in the little yellow house on Ada Lane. Billy and I visited Kelly and her grandparents recently, and she sang a duet with me when I visited with her and her church. I thought we sounded good together!

Chapter 28

The pain grew worse that year. I started having nightmares. I thought I heard someone rocking a baby in an old wooden chair, back and forth. When I got up to check it out, it was just the running washing machine. I dreamed someone left a baby on my doorstep. There was a lot of publicity then about "The Year of the Child". Someone told me I could get free therapy at the birth defect clinic, because of my condition. I sat on my step in the den after David left for school one day. *Oh, God*, I prayed. *Someone said I should be thankful for my pain, but I'm not, and you know I'd be lying if I said I was. I'm not thankful for my pain, Lord. If there's something I'm supposed to be learning from this, please reveal it to me. Are You punishing me? What have I done wrong?* Then I called the birth defect clinic and they told me that I was eligible for psychological therapy. I have since learned to be thankful not for my pain, but even through my pain.

The first day I went to therapy I was dressed in a pretty, long dress, because at that time in my life, all my dresses were ankle-length. They were beautiful -- blue, pink, yellow, light green, with puffy sleeves and lace. I felt like a princess when I wore them. They were the kind of dresses I wore when I sang at churches. A friend of mine, who worked in a beauty shop, bought me a wig of curls. At that time, I wore my hair pulled up on my head in curls. My own mother couldn't even tell when I was wearing the wig.

When I got into the therapy room, I was asked, "Why do you think you need therapy?" 'Well, I keep having all kinds of baby dreams. I think maybe I just need to talk to someone about all the things that worry me. I have so much pain now. I don't know why." "Well, dear, you have osteogenesis imperfecta, and you've had lots of broken bones. I would think that having pain would be expected. You are in your 30's now, and most people who have O.I. can't even walk. Perhaps you do need therapy. We all need someone to talk to now and then. Did you ever think you were hearing yourself crying in your dreams?" "No, I never thought of such a thing," I told her. That was when I was first introduced to Dr. Fry.

Dr. Virginia Fry was a quiet, gentle lady. "What seems to be the matter?" she asked. "Well, I don't know. It seems like everything is stacking up on me. I am so tired, and I hurt so much. I have dreams where I hear babies crying. I miss David so much since he's in school, but Loretta and Alice bring their babies over for me to babysit sometimes. You think that would help. My head hurts badly."

"When does it hurt?" she asked. "I don't know." "Well, why don't you try writing things down for me this week." "Like what?" "I'd like to know when your pain is worst." "Well, I don't know. It comes at different times of the day." "How do you write?" "I use a Braille writer and a typewriter."

"So use the typewriter so I can read it." "You know, Dr. Frye, I have so much to do. I'm not sure I have time to do this writing." "Does anyone help you?" "No". "So you take care of your little boy yourself?" "Yes, I do, and that's the job I love the most. Well, I love going to churches and telling about the Lord, too." "You look awfully pretty," she said. "Is this how you dress all the time? Please feel free to come to therapy dressed a little more casually, if you like." "I like dressing this way. It hides my crooked leg." "Boy, you worry about everything, don't you? Are you and your husband getting along OK?" "I try to make everything go smoothly, really I do." "How hard do you have to try?" she asked. "Hard. I have to be careful not to cause him to have a temper tantrum." "You cause him to have temper tantrums?" "Well, it's always because I've done something wrong that he has them." "What does he seem to get angry about?" "He gets angry if I don't have dinner on the table at exactly five o-clock. I made hamburgers the other night. He said I should have made hamburger steak with a salad. Sometime I just want a hamburger. He threw a stool at the den door the other night. The next day, David threw his train across the room. I spanked him." He said, 'Daddy did it.' Oh, I don't know, I just feel all confused." "Did your parents ever abuse you when you were a child?" "Oh, no, my parents loved me." "Well, I'm sure they loved you, but I asked if you were ever abused." "Oh, my dad only hit me one time. He hit me across the legs with his belt because I slipped off through the hedges." "Margie, there are lots of ways to be abused other than being hit." "I can't think of any," I said. "Well, did either of them ever yell at you, for instance?" "No," "Did they not get after you for anything, ever?" "Well, sometimes Mom got after me if I wasn't smiling. She'd say, 'Stop pouting, Margie. I want you to be smiling and happy. That makes other folks feel better.' And so, all my life, I tried to be Merry Sunshine for her." "Whether you felt like it or not?" she asked me. "Well, I guess so. You should be the same all the time, no matter how you feel." "So how did you feel most of the time?" "Happy, I think." "How do you feel right now?" "Well, I can't tell you how I feel, I can just tell you what I do. I can't tell you how I feel." "Why is that?" "I don't know. I just never think about how I feel." "Well, that's the first thing we have to change. How do you feel when Don is mad?" "I don't know. I just go put my arms around him and ask him to not be angry." "Margie, what makes you do that?" "I'm scared." "So you feel scared. Oh. I want you to learn how to tell me how you feel about things."

Another day Dr. Fry said, "Let's talk about you and your daddy." "What about us?" "How did you feel about your daddy?" "Ummm… how did I feel about him? Well, I guess I felt sad when he came in drinking. I felt scared when Mom would wake me up in the night." "Why would she wake you up?" "Well, if Daddy got mad at her and started to leave, she'd wake me up and say, 'Hurry, come on in here and beg Daddy not to go off. He's drunk and he might get killed.' I was just a baby, only 3 years old. So I would run into their bedroom and sit on his lap. I would beg him, 'Please Daddy don't go anywhere. Stay here with me and Mom. Take off your shoes.' I would climb down and try to get his shoes off. 'OK,' he would say. 'I'll stay home if you'll sleep with me and Mom.'" "And so did you sleep with them?" Dr Fry asked. "I did." "And how often would you sleep with them?" "Oh, I don't know. It seems like most of the time. Daddy wanted me in the middle." "So, did he sleep with his arm around you? Or did you sleep close to your mom?" "I don't remember." "How did you feel about sleeping with them?" "I don't remember. When I was older, Daddy would come to my room." "So did he sleep with you then?" "No, he would just sit on the side of my bed." "Did it scare you?" "Well, I guess I thought I was just helping keep him at home" "Did he hurt you?" "No." "Did he touch you?" "Yes." "Margie, that was abuse." "He never hurt me." "Did you know daddies weren't supposed to touch their little girls?" "Well, yes, but I had to keep him at home. He might get killed."

And so the therapy went on, and Dr. Fry grew to learn everything about me, from birth to age 43. Dr. Fry made my life different. I had never had a friend like her. I had many insights while I was in therapy, looking back on my life and learning. Don's temper tantrums were growing more frequent, and I had just about decided I was never going to be okay again, as long as I had to walk on eggshells to keep him from having temper tantrums.

   Don continued to have many temper fits when things didn't go his way, and when David was about seven, I divorced Don. We missed the good things, but we were glad to be rid of the bad things.

Chapter 29

During this time, Toni and I grew closer and closer. Sometime later Don and I decided to try being together again. He said he'd never throw another temper tantrum because he loved me so much. I really tried to believe him, even though Dr. Frye said that as a rule, after a while, it would be even worse than before. She hoped it would be different for me. Toni and Ron were still having great financial troubles, and they started coming over on Sunday to have lunch with us. She said that sometimes it was the only good meal they had for the week. This went on for about a year. Don got a crush on Toni. Ron told her, "You're going to have to let him quit hugging you. He's got a crush on you." "No, he doesn't." "Yes, he does." Then I told her the same thing, and she couldn't' believe it. That sort of put a damper on the enjoyment of it all, and even though Toni and I were still close they didn't come over every Sunday anymore.

Don promised that there would be no more temper fits, but, of course, there were. By now, David was about thirteen. One day, Don shook me by the arm, and when David came in to see if I was okay, he dropped me on the bed and grabbed David. This really scared me because he had never hurt David before. I ran outside in my gown and barefoot screaming, "Help, help! Somebody help!" My neighbors across the street came running.

They asked, "What do you want us to do?"

I said, "Make Don stop hurting David."

Scott, my neighbor's son, ran in, and Don let go of David when he heard Scott coming. Then, I left Don for good. I knew I didn't love him anymore.

About two years later, I married Bill Lane. When we moved to Maryland, Toni was the one who drove all the way up to take David and me. She said she knew the next morning that we would never make it. She didn't want to fly back without us, but I had to make sure that we couldn't make it. Bill and I were never able to work out a close compatibility. He had extreme intimacy problems and was just unreasonable in many situations.

David and I came home from Maryland and lived at Mom's house. Judy's boys were there most of the time, too. David went back to the school he had attended before we left Knoxville. I thought it was important to get him back in with his old friends. Oh, what advice I did get! Jim wanted me to take his car away because he was afraid he would get into drugs. Mom thought I should put him at Carter High School, which was nearer her house. Mom thought I should leave the door to my room unlocked, but I knew better than that. My sweet little nephews didn't understand that you weren't supposed to go in someone else's room unless invited. I had to hide Cokes under my bed in order to make sure I would have one when I wanted it! Mom was angry with me; she said I was selfish. She charged me rent, and then there was the cat. I was a woman, but I was still Mom's little girl. I was David's mom, but I was still Mom's little girl. Even though I had gone back to my safe haven, it didn't feel like a haven anymore. I got money from the sale of my home on Ada Lane, so I found David and me an apartment near his school, where we lived until he graduated. Toni helped me get it fixed up and straightened into a home – what a job! Toni and I were still as close as ever.

When David graduated from high school, Bill and I decided to try it again, this time in Johnson City. I thought that if I was closer to home, I might be able to make it with him – what a joke. So Toni again helped me turn a beautiful townhouse up on a hill into an absolutely terrific home. After that we bought a home in Johnson City and moved in. Everyone loved it and called it a charming place.

David started college at Carson Newman, and I believe he was majoring in religious education. Then we made a wise decision and moved him to Milligan in Johnson City. Milligan was a super-academic college, and when they heard that David made 4.0 on all his grades, they almost captured him, they were so glad to have him attending their college. He got all scholarships there, and when he graduated, they begged him to stay and go to their seminary. It was sponsored by the Christian denomination, and David told them that he had better get back to Baptist, as that was how he had been raised. He went to Southern Baptist Seminary in Louisville, KY, for a year and a half. That year happened to be the year that 500 students made an exodus from the Baptist seminary. There was a battle going on between the conservatives and the liberals. David found himself somewhere in the middle. He called me one night and said, "Mom, I have got to get out of here. My door looks terrible, because they have written things on it about me."

"Do you want to go to Texas Southern Baptist?" I asked.

"No. I hate changing location, so I will just go across the street to the Presbyterian seminary." He ended up graduating magna cum laude from the Presbyterian seminary.

When David left for seminary, I had stayed with Bill Lane about five more weeks, and ended up at Mom's again. *What am I going to do with the rest of my life?* I wondered. Toni could hardly believe it when I announced that I was going to Nashville. "Another move?" she exclaimed. But she was all for it, if it would make me happy – what a friend!

After arriving in Nashville, I stayed for three months with my dear friends from my old school days at TSB, Ralph and Linda Brewer. During that time I talked on Linda's phone more than she did, getting reacquainted with all my blind friends in the Nashville area, and there were a lot of them. What a wonderful thing to get my mind channeled in the right direction again by these old friends! It was like another trip through therapy, because everyone wanted to hear the stories of me and Bill Lane.

I finally found an apartment. It was so little that I called it "my little cozy". It was the first time I had lived in an apartment alone, as David had always been with me before. I made up my mind the only one I needed was God. All kinds of people lived at Parthenon Towers, and they all called me "baby" and asked if they could help me anytime they saw me downstairs, going to wash or going to the cafeteria. Toni came to visit and helped me put up pictures and arrange the furniture, so that even my treadmill found a home between the bed and the closet.

I met lots of new people and after about two or three years, I found a much nicer apartment at the Villa Marie Manor in Nashville. Not another move! But Toni put as much thought and more energy into shaping the new apartment into another safe haven. She says she only has one more move tucked away somewhere inside for me, but Ron says he's just not helping!

Chapter 30

I had only been living at Villa Marie one day when I met my future husband, Billy Hinkle. Mildred Fairbanks picked me up one day to take me to her daughter, who was the eye maker. I explained to Jeannie that I wanted my eyes to be blue, blue, blue. My cousin, Joyce, who is an artist, told me to tell Jeannie to put just a hair of gray in the blue. She wanted my eyes to be that Wiles color blue. And, so, Jeannie did exactly what we asked her to do, and my eyes are a beautiful sky blue. Everyone who sees me tells me how beautiful my eyes are. Of course, since they're mine, that makes me feel beautiful.

I told Mildred I was going to move in a week. "Who do you know over there?" she asked. "Well, no one yet, but it won't take me long to make friends." "Oh, that worries me," she said. "I have a friend who lives over there. I've gone to church with him for ages. He is the nicest thing, and that man is a caregiver." "Oh," I said. "You know, like if you needed to go to the doctor or had an emergency need of any kind, I know he would be glad to help you out." 'But, Mildred, he doesn't even know me.' "Margie, that's just the way he is," she said. "You just wait until you meet him. You'll see." "What's his name?" I asked. "Well, his name is Billy Hinkle." Little did I realize that my name would soon become Margie Hinkle.

It only took a day after I moved in before I met Billy. I went downstairs for a Valentine's party. The food was pizza; the game was penny-ante. I'll never forget that sweet little game. That was the first time I touched Billy's hand. I sure wish I had known how things were going to turn out – I would have kept that penny! We were sitting at the same table, and someone called him Billy as I took that penny from him. "Give Margie a penny, Billy." "So your name is Billy?" I asked. "Yes," he said. "You wouldn't happen to be Billy Hinkle, would you?" "Yes." "Well, my friend, Mildred, told me about you before I moved in. My name is Margie." "Well, my friend Mildred told me about you, too." "Oh, my goodness, I can't believe I met you this soon." "Me, neither. When did you move in?" "Just yesterday." And so began our romance.

I was really into working on my songs at that time. I used to go to churches and the church pianist would play for me. Things have changed in the last few years, so I started getting accompaniment tapes. They were pretty canny at first; they didn't sound real, and lots of folks called them "canned music". I would get my tapes, sit down in front of the stereo, and work and work until I could sing the song with the accompaniment tape. My friend, Sherry, came to my door one day to bring her little boy, Stephen, for his singing lesson. I loved coaching Stephen. He was a precious little 8 year old. He was a precocious little boy and loved to sing. He had lost his sight when he was about 5 years old. His older brother, Robby, was into playing ball, so Stephen wanted something of his own to do, and Sherry started bringing him for singing lessons. When Sherry came in that day, she said, "Did you know that a bunch of the little ladies were standing outside your door listening to you sing?" I wondered about getting on their nerves, but Sherry said they seemed to be enjoying it. I had often worried I was disturbing neighbors, so that put that worry to rest.

The next day, Liz Roberts and her husband, Bill, my dear friends from Knoxville, came to visit. She loved the story about Linda Ann leading me down the steep stairs at Smithwood Baptist church. I had just started going there, and her youngest daughter said, "Oh, Mama, let me lead her. I never led a blind lady, not down the stairs." "It's OK, Liz." She prayed, *Oh, hold on and don't let her fall while Linda Ann is leading her.* Liz Roberts is the same lady that David called Aunt Izza. While they were there someone knocked on the door. It was Billy. I went to the door. He said, "I thought I'd come visit you for a bit." "I would love to talk to you if you can come back later. I have company from Knoxville right now." "Of course, I'm sorry. I can come back later." When he left, I asked Liz, "How did he look? Tell me about him." "He's nice looking, Margie. Errr… Now take your time," she said. "What do you mean? I'm not interested." "Well, if you change your mind, just take your time."

The next time Billy came Sherry was back again with Stephen. "I'm giving a singing lesson now. Come in and meet Sherry and Stephen." When he left I asked Sherry, "What did he look like? Tell me about him." Sherry said, "Oh, he has hair, not bald. He's slim. He looks real nice." "That's the second or third time he's come that something is going on and I can't invite him in." Well, he wouldn't keep coming back if he wasn't interested," Sherry said. The next time I saw him it was when I called Sue, the manager of the building. I asked her, "Do you think Billy Hinkle would walk me over to Wendy's for a hamburger? I'm just dying to get outside." "You know, I really think he would enjoy that," she said. "I'll call and tell him to meet you in the lobby." "What if he doesn't want to?" "He will," she said. I combed my hair again and went down to the lobby. When he got there he said, "I had begun to think you didn't want to talk with me." "Oh, I really did," I said. "The time was just never good." "Well, today it is," he said.

When he walked with me he was so kind. He told me every crack in the sidewalk, when to step up and when to step down and finally we were at Wendy's. We ate hamburgers and drank Coke and enjoyed a good conversation. On the way back I told him, "You don't have to tell me every step. Your arm will tell me everything." "It will?" "I promise." "It's hard for me not to tell you," he said. "Your arm is telling me." Then he invited me to go to church with him on Sunday. I agreed. I went to Park Avenue for the first time that Sunday. "I know you sing, so will you go to choir with me?" I agreed. "Will you have dinner with me?" Once again, I agreed. "Oh, Margie, this is so nice. You are very enjoyable company," he said. "Will you go back to church with me tonight?" Of course! From then on, I went to Park Avenue with him, and we had dinner together each Sunday. We both loved it.

After dating for about three months, Billy said, "Let's get married."

I said, "Noooo."

"Why not?" he asked.

"Because I don't know you well enough."

"How long do you think it will take to get to know me well enough?"

"About a year." Three months later, I said, "If you really want to get married, let's do it!"

"Noooo," he said, "we're waiting a year." Then in October, my wheelchair turned over in a handicapped transportation van. It broke my pelvis in three places and crushed my shoulder joint. When I came home from the hospital, Billy came to my apartment every morning and fixed breakfast for me. "Wow," I said, "if he's this good to me before we get married, he's probably going to be a lamb after we get married." And I was right! It took a long time before I was able to walk with a walker, and another long time to be able to walk without it. When we got married I was so scared I wouldn't be able to walk up the aisle.

I did walk up that aisle on April 6, 1998, and we sat in chairs under the arch during the ceremony. I sang, "In This Very Room" to Billy. I wanted it to be the most wonderful wedding we could remember. He had had two other marriages, and so had I, but we both knew this was the one. After we got married, I kept having to use my wheelchair. *I've got to get out of this chair,* I'd think. I finally got so that I could walk when we would go out to eat. Then I broke my foot and ended up back in the wheelchair for a while. I had to build up my strength again. To this day I still struggle with my mobility. I have to use my wheelchair if there is any distance to walk. The doctors say, *Don't worry; you are doing great.* The endocrinologist gave me a wonderful compliment. He said he wished he could bottle my attitude and sell it. That made me feel good and made my Billy smile. He told the doctor that I am like that all the time. That made ME smile. Billy is a doll baby. Billy can see and has a nice car. All the blind people said, "Whoa, you married a set of wheels!" But the real truth is, I have married a sweet angel.

Before we got married, Billy went to Canada on a mission trip, and I went up to visit Mom for a week. I bought a bunch of new accompaniment tapes, so I took my recorder and Braille writer with me and wrote the words from all the tapes. I got by pretty good then. Of course, I missed Billy, and he almost scared me to death when he didn't call after he came back from Canada. I thought, *Oh dear, what's the matter? Maybe he's going to break up with me.* I called Janie and told her to call everyone she knew who might know something about Billy. She found out that Billy had come home on the plane and had reached Nashville safe and sound. I cried myself to sleep that night because I was so scared. Oh, how I loved that man! But he had just gone on to Memphis with a friend that had gone to Canada with him because the friend begged him to go. When he got back, he called to say, "I'm home now. Come on home." Ed and Judy took me home. He had had a wonderful time and told me beautiful stories about the sunset there in Canada. He told me if he ever got a chance, he wanted to go back. Sure enough, right after we got married, we found that the church was going to take people to Canada again. He said, "Oh, honey, I know we just got married, but . . ."

"Oh, I know that you told me that you wanted to go back, and I can't keep you from going." I thought, *I won't be scared we'll break up this time.* So, he took me to Knoxville, so I could visit Mom while he was gone. On Sunday, it rained and rained. I wanted to sit on the porch and read my book on tape, but there was no plug, and I had used up all my batteries. Mom just sat there and read her paper. I wanted to talk. I wanted her to talk, but I just sat there getting lonelier and lonelier. I finally took my talking book to the bedroom, put on my nightshirt, plugged it in, and read all night. *Oh, Lord,* I thought, *I'm so lonesome. I can't stand it. Why did I let him go?*

Sherrie and Cartha Lynn, who had been my neighbors on Ada Lane, took me out to lunch. That helped a little. We talked, and talked, and talked. The next day, I called Liz and said I was lonesome, and she took me to a movie. The next day, I sat around being lonesome some more, so I had Jim, Mom's friend, take me to Aunt Dorothy's. *It's never lonely there,* I thought. And she talked, and talked, and talked. I couldn't sleep there either, though. I just wanted my Billy to come home. When he did, he came straight to Knoxville. I said, "Let's go home! Let's go home!" I should have invited him to spend the night at Mom's or Aunt Dorothy's, but I just wanted to have him all to myself and get home. We started out and went home. Oh, how I love that man! He is still my angel. This one really worked. The third time is the charm.

Chapter 31

Of course, Toni and Ron still come to visit, and we go to Knoxville to visit them. Billy says, "They are good people." That's one of Billy's favorite expressions about the people he loves. So many things have happened here in this place. In 2000, David brought Rosalyn home to meet us. She had a beautiful voice, with a tiny little accent. She was a professional pianist, and Billy said she made that piano get up and walk when she played for us. Dr. Rosalyn Soo was teaching at Belmont College and had been all around the world to perform. I knew what was coming next – a wedding. Rosalyn's mom and dad were Chinese, but made their home in Canada, where Rosalyn had grown up.

I felt a little sense of fear when Billy and I were not invited to the rehearsal dinner. I had gained lots of weight and was worried that I didn't look as pretty as I had before. My legs were not as strong now, and I had to use my wheelchair more. I got a permanent and a $90.00 two-piece dress to wear for the wedding. *Oh, Lord, let me look nice for him. I don't want to be an embarrassment. Wonder why they didn't invite us to the rehearsal dinner?* Toni and Ron came down to go with us to the wedding. My wheelchair looked nice because it was brand new. Toni kept assuring me that I looked really nice. I was worried, as none of the family was coming for David's wedding. I begged Mom to come, but she had already planned a trip with the Senior Citizens. When we got to the church, David showed me where I would sit. "Just go ahead and sit here, Mom." *Whoops! I don't get to be brought in before Rosalyn's mom? I will already be sitting here, and it wasn't the front pew, either. Whoa, what's going on?* I felt shaky. The wedding was beautiful. Sherry was out of town. *Oh, Lord, I wish she was here. Maybe she could shed some light on this.*

Still, I was OK. This was my David's wedding. He would get to be with his Rosalyn the rest of his life, and I was invited to this wedding. I had forgotten to tell Billy to bring the camera, so I wondered if I would get any pictures to keep. Toni said, "Sure, you will. You know they'll send you a set of pictures." During the ceremony, there were two pastors – the one that David had been youth pastor under, and a lady pastor that Rosalyn knew. The pastor that David had worked for told the congregation that he had grown to love David like a son. He said, as a matter of fact, that he didn't have a son, so he had taken David into his heart as a son. When the ceremony was over, David said, "Mom, just stay right here. We're going out into the hall to speak to some people, and then we'll be right back to make pictures." It did my heart good to hear the smile in his voice.

All of our friends from Knoxville and different people David knew from Nashville were standing around in the auditorium talking to Billy and me. Liz and Bill had always said they were his Baptist godparents. "The only Baptist godparents in the world," Liz would say. I didn't feel left out at this point. Pretty soon, I needed to go to the restroom, so Toni went out to see if we could get my wheelchair through the vestibule with the entire crowd there. When Toni came back, I could tell she was upset. "What's wrong? Can't we get through?" "Margie they have a receiving line going on out there." "Well, the people that love David are in here." "I know, but they have a receiving line going on out there, and you're not in it. That makes me mad." "Well, it hurts my feelings, too." Liz said, "Just take her on out there and put her in the line." So Toni took me to the bathroom, and when we came out, she put me at the end of the line. However, there were only about two people left to come through the line. I don't know if it was Rosalyn's mother standing beside me or if it was her godmother. But I said, "I hope it's OK for me to be in this line." She said, "Of course, it is. I'm glad your health allowed you to be out here." So, we went back in to be there for pictures. I put on the act of my life. I felt so hurt. I felt I didn't know what was going on. *Why had they left us out of the rehearsal dinner and why didn't they want us in the receiving line? Was it David who didn't want us, or Rosalyn, or both? Lord, please help me to keep my mouth closed on this, David's wedding day. I would never want to hurt him on this special day.*

We still had to come back for the reception which was a big meal. I believe there were about 100 people in attendance. I considered whether I should go back to the reception, but I knew I had to. David had already set it up for us to be there, and he would have certainly been upset to pay for four meals and us not show up. At the reception I asked David and Rosalyn if they would send me a set of pictures. Rosalyn didn't say anything, but David said, "We should be able to handle that, Mom." To this day I have no pictures. When they came back from their honeymoon, I asked David about the rehearsal dinner and the wedding. "Why did you treat me like that?" "Mom, I let Rosalyn handle the wedding. I did it the way she wanted it." "But why wouldn't she want your parents invited to the rehearsal dinner?" "Mom, it was just for the people in the wedding." "David, you are a preacher. How many weddings have you done that left the groom's parents out?" "I'm sure there'll be plenty of them, Mom." "I don't think so. I want you to know that I am hurt that you did that to me." "Mom, why are you being so mean to me?" "Well, I didn't mean to be mean. I just wanted you to know that it hurt my heart. I'm not upset with you anymore."

Pretty soon, they moved to Jackson, GA, on the other side of Atlanta. They lived there a year or two. I tried several times to make arrangements for us to go visit them there, but something was always in the way. I guess I should have realized then that they didn't want us to come. I was living in a state of denial. My David wouldn't close me out of his life. When they moved to Mobile, AL, to take a church there, I wanted to be there for his ordination into this new church. David said, "Mom, you can't come." "David, we have the money and someone can drive us down. What do you mean, we can't come?" "Mom, I telling you, you can't come. Rosalyn is so upset at the thought of you coming, we have had to seek emergency counseling this afternoon." "What are you talking about?" I felt the top of my head start to burn. I could hardly breathe. *Oh, Lord, what's happening?* "Mom, if you come, Rosalyn said she would leave me." "She's going to leave you if I come to see you? Why? David, I don't understand. Why doesn't she want me there? I just wanted to be there for your ordination. I won't even come to your house." "Mom, I'm telling you, you can't come." "Are you closing me completely out of your life? What are you doing?" "I'll give you my cell phone number, if you make me two promises: Don't call me at home or at church, and don't come." "Please, David, please don't do this to me." "I know you won't come, Mom, because you wouldn't want to hurt me that way." "Don't you understand? You're hurting me badly. You're breaking my heart. You're my son." "I have to make a choice, Mom, and I have to choose Rosalyn." "Please tell me what I did wrong. Please, please let me apologize and ask her forgiveness for whatever I did. What is it? Tell me what's wrong." "I don't know," he said. "David, I don't believe that you don't know. Rosalyn's been your wife for two years, and if she's this angry with me, you have to know why." "I think it was something you said at the wedding." "What? What did I say?" "I don't know." "David, please tell me what I did wrong. Tell me what I said." "Are you going to make me those two promises?" "No." "NO?" I never heard David explode like that before. "Mom, I've got to go. Goodbye."

I sat on the couch, unable to cry, unable to talk. Billy slid in beside me and put his arms around me. I couldn't even tell him what had happened. I was sick. I couldn't believe what had happened. A month later, I went up and asked the church to pray about this situation. About two years later, I heard my name called. I jumped awake and knew I was dreaming. I went back to sleep only to have it happen again. *Margie. What is this? Oh, Lord, it's David.* I knew something was going on with David. I got up and got dressed and went down to our manager's office. I had sent letters to David and made several calls, but had no response. So I asked Sue, our building manager, who is a terrific counselor, to call David for me. Just see if he will talk to you and try to find out if they are OK. I know something is going on there. Sue made the call, and the church secretary said, "Oh, David is out for two weeks because of the baby." As Sue repeated aloud what the secretary said to her, I was jumping up and down, clapping my hands. Oh, they have a baby! Is it a boy? What is his name? When was he born? His name was Joseph, a sweet little boy.

Oh, to hold that baby! Rosalyn's godmother lives in Nashville. I asked them if they would try to get some pictures of Joseph for me, so my 85 year old mother could see them. They did that for me. I sent Joseph a gift for his first birthday, and it was returned, unopened. I think Billy was more shocked than me when it came back. We have Joseph's one year old and two year old pictures. I haven't had any contact with David since 2002, other than the pictures we got from Rosalyn's godparents. I pray every day that they will forgive me for whatever I've done. I am afraid to go down there. What if I went and Rosalyn left him? He would never forgive me for sure. Every day I pray, God, please fix this awful tragedy. How I love that young man. We pray that God will guide him in the leadership of his church. My whole family still hurts. We all love David so much.

Chapter 32

In 2004, I called David to tell him we had a family emergency. I left a message on the answering machine at his church. *It is Pam. I know how much you love Pam. Pammy has to have half of her skull removed. I just want you to pray. Please.* I certainly believe in prayers of love. We never heard from David. Pam still tells me that David is the last person she thought about before she drifted asleep before her surgery. Pammy has fibrodysplasia. It is a medical condition that causes the bone to thicken, which causes pressure on the brain. How I wish I could have gone to Cleveland to be with my Pammy during her surgery. Jerry, her husband, called almost every hour to keep me informed -- that sweet man. I was so glad when he and Pam got married. He's a beautiful Christian man, and Pammy is certainly at the top of his list. You can feel the love flowing when you're with those two.

"Margie," he said, on one of his calls, "Oh, Margie." "Jerry, Jerry, don't cry. Tell me, what is it?" "They snagged the lining of her brain as they lifted the skull bone. Oh, I don't know what they've done to my Pam. The damage is in the area of the speech center." I started to cry, feeling that I might never hear her sweet voice again. *Oh, God, not David and Pam both. Billy, oh, Billy.* Billy cried, too. "Tell me when she gets awake good, Jerry. Tell me if she can speak. Tell me whatever you can tell me."

Some weeks later, Pam was trying to draw pictures. She was looking for something in the mail and wanted them to check her mailbox to see if it had come. She tried drawing a mailbox and a letter. "I don't know what she's trying to say," Jerry said. "I thought about it for 24 hours, and I can't figure it out." "I got it, Margie!" he said when he called the next day. "I told her she got something in the mail, and she pointed to her pictures on the paper and nodded her head. Oh, that was a mailbox she was trying to draw, Margie." He was laughing now. "I told her we'd check that mailbox everyday. The doctors said she might have to spend six months in rehab. I'm going to take care of her," Jerry said. "'Just tell me what to do,'" I told the doctors. 'OK, take her home for two weeks then bring her back and we'll see how she's doing then.' I had to keep her walking straight. She would weave if she walked by herself." "Will she talk to me on the phone?" "No, she won't talk to you on the phone. She says she can't talk good enough yet." "Can she talk? Can she say something?" "Yes, but she stutters. She's embarrassed." "Tell her I love her. I don't care how she talks, just so she can talk."

The first time I talked to Pam on the phone, she told me that her arm was on its own. "Do you mean your arm has a mind of its own?" "Yes, my arm has a mind of its own." As far as I can tell, her arm still doesn't move like she wants it to. If she means for it to reach to the left, it will sometimes reach to the right. Because of this, she is unable to cook. She burned her arm badly once, so Jerry put his foot down and said no more cooking. They had to put a shunt in to keep the fluid on her head drained. It doesn't do the job like she wishes it could. She said it makes her head feel heavy. When they lifted the skull bones they made a mold of her skull and put in a titanium plate and two layers of some kind of medical cement. Then they rolled the skin back over it, and put in the stitches. What a miracle! Billy says her head looks normal now. We've visited them at their home on several occasions. Thank you, God, for Pammy.

Chapter 33

In early February 2008, Billy and I were sitting on the couch when the phone rang. Judy told me they had just taken Mom to the hospital. "Why?" I wanted to know. "What's wrong with her?" "She can't talk or walk or do anything," Judy answered. "What do you mean?" I asked. "Well, she got sick last night, but she didn't want to go to the hospital, so I waited until today, then I called Jerry. He and Pam came to get Mama and take her to the hospital. I'm going there now, and I'll call and tell you when we find out something." I hung up. "Oh, Billy, Mom's in the hospital. "What did Judy say?" he asked. I told him, and we sat there worrying for a while. "Oh, Billy, she's old now. She's 88. I am so worried."

After a while, Judy called back and told us they were going to keep Mom at the hospital. I found myself traveling to Knoxville the next morning with my church friend, Nancy. Our friends at the Scottsboro church have become like a family. If something's wrong, I don't have to call them – they call me. "Nancy," I asked, "are you sure it's OK for you to take off from work today?" "I've got a real good boss," she said. Billy and I both thought it was really sweet of her to do that. When we got to the hospital we called Judy and asked what room Mom was in and went straight to her room. I was afraid she wouldn't even know me. But there she sat, in a chair. "Margie Jane," she said, as I walked in the door. "Mom! Are you feeling better this morning?" "I think so," she said. "I wanna get outta here." Pam told me that Mom was mean to her the night before. They had given her Phenergan for an upset stomach. "She was so mean. She looked at me, and it wasn't her behind those eyes. It was some mean person in there." "Oh, Pam," I said, "Mom doesn't have a mean bone in her body." "Oh, yes, she does," Pam answered. "It's just been hiding. She was so mad at me. She said everything to me." I said, "Mom, if you're going to be mean to me, I'm just going home." She said, "Go ahead." I knew it wasn't her, but it still hurt me. (I'm laughing now, thinking that was funny.) So I went back in, and my friend Nancy was cutting Mama's fingernails. "I'm going to straighten up your mom's fingernails," she said. "They look like they're bothering her." "Oh, Nancy, thank you. I was whining last night that I needed something done about them." Nancy said, "Well, I'm just the gal who can do it."

Millie, Pam's friend, was there at the hospital. She said she had stayed all day yesterday with Mom. Mom had started back from when she was a very young girl and told her life story. My mouth fell open. Mom is a very private person and wouldn't tell anybody anything. "Did she talk about me?" I asked. "Of course. She talked about you and Jody and Pam and Judy." "Oh, Lord, you must have gotten an earful." Mom spoke up and said, "I told her you were the meanest one." "Mom!" I blurted out. "Mama, I was afraid you were real sick." "Oh, I was when I first got here, but I feel better today." "Mrs. Hickman," Nancy said, "do you want to get back into bed? It would be a lot softer." We realized she had been using the potty chair for a chair, which couldn't have been comfortable. A male nurse came to help her into bed, and when he left, Mom said, "He saw my behind." We laughed and told her it was OK, that he was a nurse. "He looked like a man to me," she said. Nancy raised Mom's bed up, and I climbed up there beside her. "Where are you going, Marge?" she asked. "I thought I'd come up here and love on you." Now Mom usually showed her love by buying you something. Oh, she might give you a quick hug or let you give her a very quick hug. You just felt like she wasn't comfortable with you being so close. I guess they had given her so much medicine that she forgot to be uncomfortable. I kissed her hands, hugged her, kissed her cheek. I felt really close to her. I told her I loved her. She said she loved me, too, and it felt so good. I felt closer to her than I had in a very long time. Nancy kept talking to her about everything. I know she was trying to get Mom to say something nice about me that I could remember. "Margie sure does sing pretty. I love to hear her sing alto in the choir." Mom said, "I used to sing alto." I said, "That's where I learned how to sing it." Nancy laughed and said, "I'll bet you sang pretty like Margie." Mom told her how she used to sing in the chorus at school, and I told Nancy how she used to sing in the choir at church.

I told Mom that I was going back to Nashville. Mom couldn't believe I was going back, and in truth, I had brought my clothes to stay. When I found Mom sitting up, talking, I thought that she didn't need me to stay. I really thought she'd be going home the next day. So Billy, Nancy and I headed for the car and were back home in time for church that night. On the following Monday I got so sick, I couldn't eat a bite. Pam called and said the doctor wanted to keep Mom in the hospital a few more days. By Wednesday I was feeling better, and Billy and I had plans to go to our dear friend Marie's funeral. I had known Marie Roberts since our days at TSB. The next day we went to her funeral, and while we were there, Billy became ill. He threw up twice in the restroom at the funeral home, and someone gave him a plastic bag to use on the van, which he actually used. He surely was sick. We got to our apartment, sat on the couch for a while, and Billy started to the bathroom and fell. He couldn't raise himself up with his arms. It scared me to death. I gave the on-call people a phone call, and they came and helped him up. He told them, "I'm not hurt; I just can't get up." I went and got a walker for him to use to go to the restroom, but he fell again. Anita happened to be here, and was able to help him get back up. She finally left and I got a paper cup for him. At bedtime, I brought my wheelchair to the couch and somehow we got him into it. I had to back him into the bedroom. Somehow we got him into the bed.

At 6:00 the next morning we called an ambulance. He ended up being in the hospital three days. Pam was calling me every day, telling me I had better get to Knoxville if I wanted to see Mom alive again. "I can't come, Pam, I have to get Billy well." We brought Billy home on Sunday. By Thursday he was feeling some better and had gained some strength, so I said, "Billy, go get a shower." "Why, are we going to Knoxville tonight?" I said, "Yes." He asked me to just leave him at home and go by myself. "I need you to go with me, Billy. I would worry as much about you as I'm worrying about her." So he said he would go. I really wasn't feeling good about going to Pam's house where they had taken mom when she left the hospital. Aunt Cleo had died a little over a month ago, and Pam was really ugly to me then. I had left earlier than planned that trip, feeling like I needed to get out of there. I didn't mean to go back to her house. But for Mom I told Billy I would.

Karen Villaconta took us to Cookeville, and Ron Watts, my dear friend Toni's husband, met us and took us on to Pam's house. There is a "boardwalk", as I call it, from the road down to their house. The last time I walked it , I had gotten sick to my stomach, it was so hard. Pammy said I needed to "get tough". "So," I said, "Ron, I thought I'd never walk this boardwalk again. I just don't know if I can." "Well, then," he said, "I'll walk you down in the wheelchair." I almost cried. "Do you think you can?" "I don't think I can; I know I can." So he rode me down the boardwalk. You go about two feet, then down a step, two feet, then down another. He acted like he did that everyday. When we went in the house, he rolled me right up to Mom's bed, which was in the living room. Pam said, "It's about time you got here. I almost gave away your bed." Then she laughed, and I though maybe things would be OK. Pam was trying to get Mom to wake up. "It's OK," I said, "let her sleep." "No, I want her to wake up and see you're here." I held her hand and said, "Hey, Mom, I came back to see you here at Pam's house." When I got up to go to the restroom, I heard her say, "Margie Jane," and I knew she knew I was there and it made the trip worth it all.

I felt like the medicine was making her sleep. They had already called in hospice, and they were giving her morphine. When I went back in to her bed, she reached up and touched my hair. "Your hair," she said, "it has grown." "Yes, it's grown. Do you think I should cut it?" She just laughed. I thought she would probably tell me to just roll it. When I was a little girl she used to make me eleven Shirley Temple curls. She wouldn't even let me go to a birthday party unless she had those curls fixed. She went back to sleep and we sat around the bed all night and talked. I thought the three of us were closer now than we have been in a long time – Judy, Pam and me. We sat there around her bed for two weeks. Every few days my Billy would say, "Can't we go home and come back?" I felt he was really stressing but every time I mentioned going home, Jerry would say, "Hospice says it won't be long. I wouldn't go if I were you." So we'd stay a couple more days.

All the time Pam was working on an obituary. I think she went through five different drafts. She would put people in and take people out. My David, who has been away from the family for five years, was originally included in the obituary. "I'm not putting Aunt Polly in," Pam said. "Pammy, please put Aunt Polly in," I begged. "Uncle Tom will be so hurt. He's the only member of her family left alive. Why would you want to hurt him?" "I think Aunt Polly's nosy, and therefore, I don't like her, and she's not getting in the obituary." "I hope you'll change your mind," I said. Judy said, "I want my name to be Judy Blendeen Hickman Lawson." "I'm not doing the whole obituary over to get your name right." "Well, you should have asked me before you did it." "This makes the fifth time I've done it, and I'm not doing it again." "Read it from the top," I said. She said, "Mama was preceded in death by her husband, Raymond." "What about my daddy?" I said. "Who wants your daddy in there?" she said. "Well, he belongs in there." "This obituary is going to be the way I want it." "I believe you're supposed to put the sisters and brothers who are dead and their surviving spouses." "Well, I'm not," she said. "I'm putting Sarah and Chad as her grandchildren." "Well, I'm sure you should," I said. "I think she thought of them as her grandchildren, as much as she loved Jerry." Chad's wife's daughter had a little baby, and Pam said, "I am putting Amaya Hope Ray in as Mama's great grandchild." I just sat there saying, "Duh."

"I'm putting longtime friends in, too," Pam continued. "I think Millie should have an honorable mention." "Fine," I said, "put in Millie and Willie. I don't know how we could have managed without their help." Mom had some good friends. Sylvia Easterday was Mom's Sunday school teacher, and Mom loved her very much. Mrs. Mildred Wolfenbarger was 94 years old and Preacher Wolfenbarger was our pastor for many years. Francis Sellers was a lady who lived down the road. She would come to see Mom almost every day. Mom would be nice while she was there, and when she left, Mom would say, "Whew. I'm glad she's gone." I didn't think they should put her name in there.

Chapter 34

Mama died on Saturday, March 1. All three of us girls were close by her bed, touching her and crying. I thought, *It's been so long since I really talked to her.* She couldn't hear well, and so I tried to talk in very short sentences, and only tell her half of what I really wanted to say. I'm so glad I got to tell her how much I loved her. I'm glad she's in heaven and didn't have to lie and suffer for a long time. How we'll miss her! The family will break up after this, I'm sure. They say let love go, and if it comes back to you, it was yours, but if it doesn't, it never was.

I immediately called Ron and Toni. "Mom has gone to heaven," I said. "Can you come and get me and take me to tell little Jody?" "Sure," they said, "we'll be right there," as if 30 miles was just across the street. Oh, what friends! When we got to Jody's apartment, her caregiver said, "Jody's still in bed. She won't get up for anybody." "I'll bet she'll get up for me," I said. "I'll bet she will, too. She loves you!" Toni, Ron, Billy and I all went into Jody's room. "Hi, little Jody," I said. Not a peep. "Jody's mad at me," I told Toni. About two weeks before Jody had hurt her little foot. In trying to understand about Mom, she said that Mama got hurt and was bad off sick. "No, no, Jody," I said. "Mama didn't get hurt." "Yes, she did," Jody yelled. "Ok, Ok, Jody, I'm sorry. If you want to say she got hurt, that's just fine." And so, she was still mad at me – would not say a word. I went over to her bed, kicked off my shoes, and slid under the covers with her. I started kissing her on the cheeks and the forehead. "I love you, little Jody. Don't be mad at me. I really love you." "You love me, don't you, Mahgie?" "I certainly do." "I'm afraid you're going to hurt my foot, Mahgie." "No, I won't hurt your foot. I know where it is, and I'll be careful." And up from that bed she raised.

"Jody, I came to tell you something." I put my arms around her and pulled her close to me. "Jody, you know Mama was bad off sick. You know she was really sick." She said, "She was bad off sick and went to heaven." I sat there with my mouth open. "Yeah, that's right, Jody. She went to heaven to be with Jesus just a little while ago. And now, she won't hurt anymore, and she'll be all well." "And then she can come back and live in her house on Osborne Road?" "No, my Jody, when you go to heaven you can't come back; you have to stay. You know, do you remember when Daddy T.B. was bad off sick and died and Grandma Clevenger was bad off sick and died? You know, how they went to heaven and didn't come back?" "I want to go to heaven and see my little Elma Mama," she said. "Jody, please don't say that. We're going to have a church service for Mama, and we'll sing songs for her. What do you want to sing for her?" "In the Sweet By and By," she said, without any hesitation. "And we shall meet on that beautiful shore." "That's right," I said. "I want to go see God and Jesus and Mr. Holy Ghost." And through my tears came laughter. "Oh, my Jody, I'm so glad I have you." And so I left and went back to Pam's.

On Sunday morning, we all got up and got ready to go to the funeral home to make the arrangements. We chose a blue casket with a faint blue lining. I was afraid the blue in her pretty blue dress would clash with the lining, but Karen said the lining had such a faint hint of blue that it all blended together. We put a pair of pretty twisty beads on her neck. We asked for doves to be put in the lid of her casket. The spray of flowers on her casket was made of lilies, roses and other flowers. The girls said carnations were everywhere at funerals, and they didn't want them on Mom's casket.

After we took care of that, the funeral director said, "Let's see about the obituary. Read over it, girls, and make sure it's just like you wanted." Judy started reading it out loud so I could hear. She was trying to be nice, but what a mess she got herself into. "Chad, Sarah, Howard, Sam are the grandchildren." *Here's everyone but David. Wonder why David is not in here?* I knew without asking that Pam was very angry with David, because he didn't show up before Mom died. Neither did he show up afterwards. I was not expecting him to show. If something had held him away this long, nothing would bring him back, except to solve the problem. "When did you take David's name out, honey?" I got no answer. "When did you take David's name out, Pammy?" No answer. "Look," I said. "David is still legally my son and still legally Mama's grandson, and he has the right to be in Mom's obituary." "I think you took it out," Jerry spoke up, "just after your mom died, didn't you?" "Well, he's my son," I said. A little louder: "I'm ashamed he didn't come." A little louder: "I'm sorry. But he still belongs in the paper in the obituary." "Margie, you're going to have to leave. I'm not putting up with any more of this from you," Pam said. As I yanked my cell phone out of my bra, everyone in the room gasped, because I looked so angry.

I called Ron, my friend Toni's husband. I thought to myself, *How many times during my life have I done this?* "Hello, Ron, this is Margie." "Hi, Margie." "Ron, come and get me and Billy at Pam's house." "OK," he said. Not a question, and we knew he'd be right there. What a friend. "So when is 'How Great Thou Art' from my CD going to be put in the service?" "We're not putting it into the funeral." "Why not? That's the first thing I asked for. I want that to be my gift to Mama." "You got to choose a song," Jerry said. "So unchoose it," I said. "I'd rather have 'How Great Thou Art'." No one told me it wouldn't get played if I chose a song. "Margie, hush," Pam said. "Don't you tell me to hush." By then I knew I had lost my cool, and I didn't even care. I was hurting from the loss of Mom and from the meanness in Pam. "Margie, let's wait until we get home to discuss this," Jerry said. "If I had been told about the obituary at home, it would have already been discussed at home," I said. "OK," I yelled, "leave it out! Leave it out." The more they tried to get me to hush in their embarrassment, the more I didn't care.

We went back to Pam and Jerry's house. They had dinner on the table, as folks had brought in food. The food had been brought in by Sarah's friends. I guess Billy must have been hungry. He said, "Are you going to eat?" I said, "At their table – no." He said, "I am. I'm hungry." I gathered our clothes as fast as I could, and since Billy was already eating I thought I might as well, too. About that time Ron came to pick us up. Not a soul spoke to him when he came in. "I went and bought a new mattress and springs for you to sleep on. I figured you needed your rest." "Ron, you didn't have to do that." "Well, we wanted to." Thank you, Lord, for friends.

When we arrived at Toni and Ron's house, I was wound up, wanting to talk about Mom, wanting to tell about Pam, filled with thanks that they had rescued us. "Toni, I've got to tell you about Mom." "OK, talk away, I'm ready to listen," she said. "Toni, on Wednesday night before Mom died on Saturday, she had been unable to move her arms and legs for almost the whole two weeks we were there. Just as we were ready to go to bed and sleep a little while before we had to get up, Mom raised up all by herself. She looked up, eyes wide open, held up her arms, and said, 'God!' Oh, Toni, I really believe that she saw the light of God. I think things like that happen to let us know it's real. I believe with all my heart that Mom is in heaven. She talked to her two sisters. 'Dorothy, can you stand up?' Aunt Dorothy had lain on the couch for a year before she died, although her mind was just fine. She was unable to walk at all. Aunt Cleo had died the month before Mom. 'Cleo! Cleo, wait for me!' Doesn't that give you cold chills, Toni?" "Yes, it does. Just remember, Margie – 'Vengeance is mine,' saith the Lord. Try to get the things that happened between you and Pam out of your mind. You don't have to take care of this… He will." "I know I need to pray about it but I just can't. God knows my heart, and I should be able to talk about it out loud, but I'm not." Let me tell you, readers, it was the first of May before I was able to pray about myself and Pammy.

We had our first real night's sleep that night. There was no need to wake up and check on Mom. We would have the funeral on Tuesday night, so everyone would have the chance to see the obituary in the newspaper. I called Neva and Don that morning to let them know where I was. They had been friends for so long and had come to see Mom on the Saturday before she died. "She died on Saturday," I told them. "The obit will be in the paper this morning. I am at Toni's house. My sister, Pam, asked me to leave, and so I did." "So was Mt. Harmony where your mom went to church bringing food to your mom's house?" "Yes," I answered. "Do they know you're not there?" "Yes. It might not have been nice, but I told them. I knew Mom's close friends would wonder where I was." "Well," Neva said, "give me directions to Toni's house. Someone should bring dinner to where you are." I cried. "Tell Toni Piney Grove church will be providing a meal for today." And so they brought meat, vegetables, angel food cake, fruit. It was all so delicious. For some reason, I felt like eating that night.

My sweet friend, Karen, who says she's my daughter, drove up from Nashville the next day and was there to go to the funeral with us. When we got there, I went up to the casket and knew that my mom would be the first dead person I had ever touched. I touched her sweet little hands, her face, her hair, and the pretty twisty beads. *Yes, she's beautiful, like a big lady doll.* There were no tears, just numbness. Jerry had given me back the CDs I had made and given Pam as a gift. He said, "Take care of this yourself." So I asked the funeral director if he would put one of them on at 7:30 and let it play until 8:00. That would be my gift. When the CD started to play, Jody got quiet as a mouse. "Are you OK, Jody?" I asked. "I love to hear Margie's voice," she said. Oh, that precious girl, how she picked me up when I was down. Karen said, "Boy, she sure is listening." I asked Brother Bob Bevington if I could talk about Mom when she was young, when Jody and I were little. "Talk it over with the family," he said. "But the family isn't speaking to me." "Well, then, don't do it. You'll be pouring gas on the fire." I was so hurt. There was hardly anything said about Mom. Of course, I know it was more important to talk about Jesus, but it was Mom's funeral. Oh, well, what do I know?

Sadly, Pam, Judy and their families sat in the back, and we were all in the front. No one spoke to me except my nephew Sam when we came in. He came and kissed me on the cheek, just like always. When they started to sing "In the Sweet By and By," little Jody's lips began to move. I started singing alto, very softly. Soon, others joined in and the whole room filled with song. It was wonderful.

I remembered the dream Mom had last summer. "Margie," she told me, "I dreamt last night that Jody was in heaven." "Oooh," I said. "She was so cute, she was three feet tall just like now, but her little legs were straight and she had on black patent slippers with a little strap like I use to buy you. She was dancing all over some street. Do you think that means something's going to happen to her? I don't know, but it sure was real." How strange. It was Mom who went to heaven, not Jody. Every time Jody and I talk since Mom died, she tells me how she wants to go to heaven and live with her little Elma mama. "Is Charlotte Ann in heaven, Margie?" "No, she's on earth." "Is Joyce Ellen in heaven?" "No, she's on earth." "Are Jackie Pickle and Alvin Wiles in heaven?" "Jody, all the cousins are still here." I didn't want to explain that Alvin had been killed in Viet Nam. "Joyce Ellen is on the athe?" "No, Jody, *earth*." She had never said "athe" before. "Say 'earth'." "Eff," she said. I didn't realize we had never taught her to say earth. I guess there had been no reason to.

Chapter 35

Billy and I left on Wednesday morning right after the burial to return to Nashville with Karen. "I'm so tired," he said that night. He went over to Wendy's to get us chili for supper. "Ooh, it's so good to be home." "I know, darling'," I said. "It is good to be home, but it sure feels like the world is an emptier place." I can't believe all the sisters are gone in a year. They were the backbone of the family. Joyce Ellen called and we cried. The next morning Billy let me sleep until he called to me, "Come here, honey, I need you." I jumped out of bed. I was scared. "Oh, honey, what is it? What's wrong?" "I can't fix the breakfast." "What part of the breakfast can't you fix?" "I can't put it together. And I dropped the coffee pot." "Oh, Lord, did it burn you?" "No, but I can't pour any more in my cup." "Why can't you pour it?" "I don't know. Just pour it for me, and put my biscuit together." "OK, honey, but what's wrong? You sound funny when you talk." "I can't help it." "Oh, I didn't mean you should help it, I just meant what's wrong?"

He sat there on the couch and didn't move. "Can you come to the table or should I hold it for you right there?" "I'll come to the table." "Billy, I think you should go to the doctor. I think we should take you to the doctor now." "No, I'm going to eat my breakfast." "Well, yeah, eat your breakfast, and then we'll go. We'll go to the emergency room." "Oh, no, we won't," he said. "I'm not sitting in that emergency room three or four hours." "So, we'll go to Dr. Calish's office."

At Dr. Calish's office I said, "Listen, he isn't saying his words plain." "I'm sorry," he said. "No, no, don't be sorry. I'm just trying to explain that something has happened to your speech." "I'm writing up orders," the doctor said. "You'll need to go to the emergency room." "No," said Billy. "I'm not going." "But, Mr. Hinkle, you have to go the emergency room so they can do an MRI." So down to the emergency room, that unloved place, we ended up. Even though she had written orders we sat there for an hour and a half and stayed in the hospital three days. The doctors were unable to find traces of a mini-stroke but were sure he had had one. He was so weak and continued to have slurred speech. When we came home we worked on each of the words he would say differently. He has them all back now. So far, he is doing fine again.

Chapter 36

On April 9, 2008, I found myself in Chancery court in Knoxville. Five years ago I went to Knoxville with the paralegal who had had Aunt Cleo's name taken off Mom's conservator papers and mine put on. Those sweet little sisters thought I was trying to do something bad to them. With Mom 83 and Aunt Cleo 88, I guess I could understand why they would think I was taking advantage of them, but I would never do that. Hadn't they known me all 68 years of my life? Aunt Cleo cried and said if Mom wanted her off the papers, she would sign her name to get off, but if Mom didn't want her off, she would stick there tight as glue. "Mom, it's just that Aunt Cleo is older than you, and someone needs to be on Jody's conservator papers with you who could take over if something happened to you." "I'm not ready to die," she said. "I reckon I'll be here for a while." "Mom, if you'd rather someone else was on the papers…." "I'm not going to argue with you," she said. "Have it your way." "Don't be mad, Mom."

That was the last I heard of those papers. They were lost. No one seemed to know where they were, until Mom passed away March 1, 2008, and the legal advocate called me two or three days later, telling me that she had Jody's conservator papers. They had been at the bottom of a stack in one of the lawyer's office. I wasn't feeling like conservator papers that day, and I made that little girl cry.

Anyway, there I was in Chancery Court, trying once again to get on Jody's conservator papers, because as of now, she had no conservator. The judge was saying, "I have no proof that this girl needs a conservator." "This is her sister," said the lawyer. "I can't help it if it's her mother. I have no paper proof. You know I have to have proof." "So, what should I do?" *Uh-oh*, I thought, *we're in trouble. This silly lawyer doesn't know he's supposed to bring proof.* "Go get a medical statement," the judge told him. "Well, can I at least swear her sister in so she doesn't have to rush back up here each time we need her?" "Certainly," said the judge. He asked me about six questions and said they would bring the papers the next week. Well, that was pretty easy, but in my heart I knew it wasn't. He hadn't even known the judge would need paper proof.

I went out and spent the afternoon with little Jody. She was missing Mama badly. She said she wanted to go to heaven and live with Mama Elma. "Jody, I can't handle that right now. You have to stay here on the earth with me for a while." "What did you say, Margie? I'm going to stay here on the 'aith' with you?" Becca, one of the caregivers, came in and asked her if she'd like to go to church, since it was a Wednesday night. "I do," she said. A few minutes afterwards, Ron picked me up to take me back to Cookeville where I met Karen for the rest of the trip back to Nashville.

Judy was still living in Mama's house, since Mama asked for her to stay until Sammy graduated from high school. Jerry took a big truck and moved Judy and all of Mama's furniture into Judy's house that she had been renting for a year and a half. My heart skipped a beat as I knew she would never make it financially. In July 2008 I returned to Knoxville where Jody's personal companion, Aola, Jody and I went to lunch together at Shoney's, where they treated Jody like royalty. They thought she was doll, which she is! Aola takes her there quite often. She dresses her in beautiful dresses from J. C. Penney's. Jody's favorite foods which she eats every time she goes are good ol' soup beans, greens, chopped up onions – good and cold – and chopped up tomatoes. Boy, does she eat! We didn't get fudge cake that day, as I had brought her a peanut butter pie we were going to eat at home. I spent the night with her and slept on an air mattress at the foot of her bed. Mom had planned and planned to do this with Jody and never did. I wish somehow I could bring Jody some comfort and let her know I want her to lean on me.

The next day we got up, got ready and went to the movies together. *Hey,* I thought, *this is like real, normal sisters.* We saw "Mama Mia". I think I've said before that Jody has an obsession with bottle and purses. She had played in her pocket book full of bottles I brought for her all night long and fell asleep in the movie. When we got home she was wide awake. She wanted to play the piano. She played a melody and even added chords. "What are you playing, Jody?" I asked. "What's the name of that tune?" "Up and Down", she answered. I giggled. She was having a ball, just playing up and down.

By the middle of August 2008, the family was about to disown me because I had no conservator papers for Jody which would allow the property to go into probate court. "Billy", I said, "I knew I would have to fight before this is over. I can't do it as well as I did when I was young." "You can do it, though," he said. I started out on Monday morning, bound and determined to find that lawyer and tell him a thing or two. I even called someone from the State. None of us could reach him. Speaking of the paralegal, CP, Community in Action and I have called and called and called. That scoundrel wouldn't answer the phone for any of us. Boy, he answered when the lady from the State called him, and he called me bright and early the next morning. I believe it will go through now. The property can't go through probate, be sold and close without me being able to sign for Jody. Why does everything have to be so hard? And now Judy is losing her car. How sad. It's only been a week ago that she asked if she could move back into Mom's house until it is sold. She is in deep financially. Bless her heart. I wish we could help, but we can't. There's no telling what will happen to those three – Judy, Sam and Howard – but they are in my prayers each day. I believe I will receive the conservator papers. I believe the house will sell. I believe God will take care of all of us. And I believe this is about the end of my story.

Letters

The following are letters that were given to Margie by a few of her dear friends.

October 13, 1976

When Margie asked me to write about a particular event in our friendship that stood out in my mind, I could think of nothing.

What I think of Margie is a blur of a thousand telephone calls over a period of years. We became very close over the phone. I always knew I could count on her to cheer me up when I was down, for emergencies when I needed help with the children, and always with concern for me.

How can one describe a best friend? We have laughed together, cried together, been everywhere in Knoxville together and even spanked our children together. She was with me through the ordeal of my husband's battle with Hodgkin's Disease. She was there during the many times my little girl was hospitalized and finally the death of my father-in-law. If there is any description of a best friend, these are the things that count. She prays for you, calls to cheer you and is always there with a smile. I love her for being such a friend and will never have another quite like Margie.

Loretta Miller

What is a Margie Mauldin? Well, she's 99 ¾% pure friendship. I would say 100%, but then someone might think I was a little prejudiced! She's my friend, but then she's "friend" to many people. So that's not unusual. Many people are that. She's blind, but that's not unusual. Many people are blind. So, what's unusual about a Margie? Maybe—the fact that she can see—I forget that she's blind because she "sees" so well. I do dumb things like turning on the car lights so she can see to count her money, or walking off and leaving her standing in a store, fully expecting her to follow—which she usually does. You see we both have the same "affliction"—we talk a lot and she can follow my voice as well as my noise!

Margie and I have been through many joys and many sorrows. It always seems that when I need her she's up and when she needs me, I'm up. I know our worse time was when Margie and Don were applying to adopt and old naïve Liz, just couldn't believe that anyone couldn't see what a beautiful loving home they have. How capable, But . . . and boy! That is a big word. The world is cruel, as we found out, and we had some rocky, trying times. I was hurt and I hurt my friend by lack of faith. Hopefully, I've grown "much" since then, we also have learned a hard lesson. Talk it out! Don't sit home and cry! Doesn't accomplish anything but swollen eyes and nose!

I cannot in all my honesty, imagine my life without Margie, Don and David. I guess they're part of my family and without them I'd be much less than complete.

So what is a Margie Mauldin? A faithful Christian, a loving wife, an adoring but firm mother and friend! For this I give thanks and pray that God will continue to bless Margie and all her family and friends.

Liz Roberts

I don't remember when I met Margie. I can't imagine what life would be like without her. Sure, she's blind, but to anyone who knows her, she is more sighted than most people with two eyes.

I babysit with David and he is really talented. Margie spends so much time with him, teaching him so much, and even with a five year old running around, her house is usually spotless.

Also I help Margie get her music together and indexed for her concerts. I really love to do things for her because I love her and her family.

Margie is more than just a friend, she is also there to help whenever you need a question answered. Once in Sunday School, I was asked, "Who has made the biggest impression in your life?" I said Margie. She's more than wonderful, she's even almost great!

Linda Roberts
Age 16

As I look back over my friendship with Margie I can see how God had enriched my life by me knowing her.

The first time was in Liz Robert's Sunday school class at Smithwood Baptist Church. I came in the room and there sat a lady wearing the ONLY smile. She was smiling inside as well as outside. After meeting all the member of my class, I really didn't want to be friends with anyone except, Margie. By saying that I didn't want to be friends with anyone I wasn't ready for rejections. You see I didn't want anything from them, but I wanted them to accept me and to love me.

I knew that Margie was blind so I thought to myself that this is one person that I could give myself to. She couldn't see, and that made me feel a little more secure about giving myself away. I really wanted this friendship.

As I kept seeing her at church and talking to her from time to time I knew I loved her. At first, when we would go shopping I would feel a little nervous about leading her around, I really didn't know if she would enjoy doing the things that I did. I'll never forget the day when she asked me if she made me nervous by going places with her, and if she did we could no longer have a friendship. I was hurt, but I didn't let that stop me from praying about our friendship. I talked to Liz Roberts about our little problem, and she encouraged both of us to pray about this misunderstanding.

For a while I didn't know how she felt about wanting our friendship to grow. The Lord whispered in both of our hearts that we have both been blessed by knowing each other. Margie is very special to me now, not only is she a friend at our church, but a sister in Christ.

She has shared the love she has for Jesus Christ with me many times, and that ministers to me so much. I'll never forget the first concert she gave at Smithwood Baptist Church that I saw. There she was in a very beautiful long dress, her hair in curls all put on top of her head.

I came expecting to hear a good religious program filled with praise for the Lord, but it was much, much, more that that! She sang from her heart and the Lord filled her with His Spirit! The whole church was overjoyed with her concert. I never realized how really good she did sing until that night, you see she didn't do it, the Lord did it! I praise the Lord for the memories of our friendship for you see this is by no means an end of a story but the beginning of more beautiful memories.

In Christ,
Bernice Julian

God answered a prayer, when he sent Margie into my life. She and I have never doubted that's why our relationship is special. Created by the Lord. Now, that's exciting, or at least we thought so!

Margie didn't seem at all surprised when I told her of my request to the Lord for a Christian friend. And that I thought she was the answer.

Now this may seem rather silly to you. Praying for a friend. You might say—it's just not that way for me. I happen to be on the shy side, and it is exceedingly difficult for me to talk to people. Yet the need to share and become friendly is my desire. Margie sensed this without my coming right out and saying so, from the very beginning.

It seemed from the moment we met, it was instant friendship. That first day I spent with her, we nearly talked each others ears off.

Now you might wonder just how I would react to my friend being blind. Well, I'll tell you I was scared to death! But I tried so hard not to let it show. Margie was and still is patient with me. And I'm learning!

The first lesson is, "Don't treat me blind! You don't have to tell me to take a step here or there. I'm holding your arm, and it will tell me when to step. And don't worry about my bumping into things, I'm blind, and used to it!"

"Well, all right," I said, "if you are sure."

She is so confident and in charge. Sometimes I forget that she's blind. Because she does see. Maybe not with eyes. But with God given sight that listens, and feels things in a way my eyes have yet to see.

Oh I've learned so much from my God given friend. My Christian sister. She gives so much of herself to others. She's a walking, talking, singing witness to everyone she meets.

Each time I hear her sing, my life is renewed. She gives me courage and strength as a Christian. Her testimony never seems to get old. But blossoms with each telling, as fresh spring flowers.

Yes, I admire her! For she is truly dedicated in service for our Lord and Saviour.

I hold our friendship in highest esteem. And our prayer life as sacred. For having a prayer partner such as Margie has been a great blessing.

A few years ago, I decided that I really wanted to do something special for Margie, something to fulfill a need. So I confronted her by asking if I would be of help in doing some correspondence for her. She said, "Oh! That's an answer to my prayer. I've needed for so long to have someone help me send my posters and announcements to the churches I visit."

Well, I was delighted. And we began to work right away. And I love every minute of it. This I thought was helping myself to get involved in something really worth the time and effort.

So now, Margie calls me her secretary, and someday I hope to live up to the meaning of that word.

Margie also babysits my three children. They adore her, especially my daughter Jennifer. It's always a very special treat for her to visit Margie's house. And the love they share is so beautiful. But Margie loves all the kids. She's a natural mother. And little ones respond to her in a way that fascinates all who watch on. Her light shining brought as a beacon, as the scripture says.

"Don't hide your light! Let it shine for all; let your good deeds glow for all men to see, so that they will praise your heavenly Father" (Matthew 5:15-16, Living New Testament).

Alice Holbrook
Knoxville, TN 37917

I was nervous about the daunting task of helping a woman to write her autobiography. What if I don't ask the right questions? What if she doesn't like me? As I knocked on Margie's door for the first time, I took a deep breath. "Come in!" she hollered. I walked through the door, and I knew in my heart that Margie and I were going to be friends. I was delighted to find out that she was a Christian, which gave us an immediate connection. After that first visit, I called my mom and told my friends about how excited I was to be doing the project with Margie. That excitement never dwindled. I looked forward to meeting with Margie every week, and we always had the best time together, laughing at her stories and talking about life. I could not have asked for a better experience. I am grateful to Margie for allowing me to come into her life, which was a great risk on her part. She never held back. Margie has shared her true self, which has made me feel like a true friend. I thank God for Margie's life and all the people He has touched because of her willingness to serve Him. I have been blessed by knowing her.

Bonnie Holmes
April 29, 2006

Margie Hinkle is a 69 year old miracle. She can style her hair better than I can my own. She can wrap a gift, hem a skirt, prepare a dinner. She is independent and assertive, well-spoken and entertaining. She has learned how to use a computer. She somehow understands all about colors. She suffers from a great deal of pain and discomfort due to her conditions, but she is always bright and cheerful. All this with never having seen a thing and never having a strong body.

Margie has been a great friend to me and a wonderful part of my life, as well as my son's. She brought him many hours of happiness through the years, and I will be forever grateful for her love for us.

Now Margie has written a book about her life, and we are excited it is finally finished. She thinks her story might be an inspiration to others. So do I.

Sherry B. Hatchett
Nashville, TN
September 2009